The FOUR GIFTS of LOVE

Other books by Willard F. Harley, Jr.

His Needs, Her Needs
Love Busters
Five Steps to Romantic Love
Give and Take
Your Love and Marriage

The FOUR GIFTS of LOVE

Preparing for Marriage That Will Last a Lifetime

WILLARD F. HARLEY, JR.

Fleming H. Revell
A Division of Baker Book House
Grand Rapids, Michigan 49516

Published by Fleming H. Revell
a division of Baker Book House Company
P.O. Box 6287, Grand Rapids, MI 49516-6287

Printed in the United States of America

Library of Congress Cataloging-in-Publication Data

Harley, Willard F.
      The four gifts of love : preparing for marriage that will last a lifetime /
Willard F. Harley, Jr.
          p.   cm.
      ISBN 0-8007-1754-6 (cloth)
      1. Courtship—Psychological aspects. 2. Marriage—Psychological aspects. 3. Communication in marriage. I. Title.
HQ801.H3273   1998
306.73'4—dc21   98-9232

For current information about all releases from Baker Book House, visit our web site:
http://www.bakerbooks.com

CONTENTS

One

A LIFETIME OF LOVE

You will exchange rings on your wedding day. These rings symbolize your commitment to love and care for each other—your gifts of love. But do you really understand what you are promising to do for each other? And is it something you intend to do every day for the rest of your life?

You have probably given each other the gifts of love throughout your courtship. That's why you have fallen in love. If you continue to give them, you will be as much in love throughout your marriage as you are on your wedding day. But if you stop giving them, as so many couples do, your love will be lost and your marriage will be threatened.

I have devoted my life to saving marriages and have helped thousands of couples avoid the pain and disaster of divorce. Couples usually see me when they are just about ready to throw in the towel. But when they learn to give each other the four gifts of love, the wedding gifts that they should have given to each other at the time of their wedding, the threat of divorce is ended.

What a pity that these couples did not begin their marriage the right way! They thought the love they felt for each other on their wedding day would carry them through life, regardless of what they did. They didn't realize that without the four gifts of love, they would actually lose their love for each other. And without love, their dream of a fulfilling marriage would become a nightmare.

Love Keeps Marriages Healthy

How did you and your partner decide to marry? Did you discuss the pros and cons of your lifelong marriage with friends and relatives? Did you take a test to determine if you are compatible? Did you find that you each meet objective criteria that predict marital success?

Maybe you did some of these things, but I doubt that they had much effect on your decision to marry. Most couples marry each other because they are in love and cannot imagine living without each other. They marry because they find each other irresistible.

That's how it was for me and my wife, Joyce. Long before I asked her to marry me, we both knew that we could not possibly be happy without each other. I was in love with her and she with me. We enjoyed being together, spent part of every day with each other, and talked together for hours at a time. This had been going on for years before we were married.

We broke up a few times and dated others, but whenever that happened, we missed each other terribly. We eventually realized that life without each other would be a tragic mistake, and so to avoid disaster we married much sooner than we had originally planned. Joyce was only nineteen; I was twenty-one.

Thirty-five years later, with two married children and four grandchildren, we still cannot imagine what life would be without each other. And we still find each other irresistible.

But Joyce and I don't have a good marriage because we were meant for each other. It might seem that way, but it isn't true. The reason we have a good marriage is because, over the years, we have done things for each other that have kept our love strong. We have given each other the four gifts of love.

Before I tell you about these gifts and how they can guarantee the success of your marriage, I want you to understand how love works. What is it that made you fall in love with each other? What could cause you to lose that love? To help me explain this important concept to you, let me introduce you to the Love Bank.

The Love Bank

Most people regard the feeling of being in love as one of life's great and wonderful mysteries. The feeling of love is certainly great and wonderful. But it's not a mystery. In fact love is quite predictable. It's that predictability that makes my job possible. I help married couples rediscover love for each other after it's been lost. To help them, I must not only know how love is lost, but I must also know how it can be recovered.

To help my clients understand how predictable love is, I have invented the concept of the Love Bank. It helps me explain how love is created and how it is destroyed.

There is a Love Bank inside each one of us. Every person we know has an account in our Love Bank and it keeps a record of how they treat us. If a person makes us feel good, love units are deposited into that person's account. The better we feel, the more units are deposited.

However, if that person makes us feel bad, our emotions withdraw love units from his or her account. The number of units withdrawn depends on how bad we feel.

The Love Bank

The Love Bank is the way our emotions keep track of how people treat us. Good experiences deposit "love units," leading us to like or even love a person. Bad experiences withdraw units, leading us to dislike or even hate a person.

It's possible to make someone fall in love with you. First, you must determine what it is that makes the person feel good and then you learn to do it for him or her. The better you can make that person feel, the more love units you will deposit until you have reached a threshold, say one thousand love units, where one more love unit creates the feeling of romantic love. Of course, if your account ever drops one love unit below that threshold, the other person's feeling of love for you will evaporate, so it makes sense to build a cushion, well above the romantic-love threshold. Otherwise, it won't be love at all, just infatuation—love that's here today and gone tomorrow.

So that's how to win someone's heart: Learn how to make that person feel so good that your love bank account breaks through the love threshold. The reason someone is in love with you today is because you have learned to do just that.

However, it's not only possible to make someone love you, it's also possible to make someone hate you. All you need to do is make the person miserable. That empties the Love Bank and then continues to withdraw love units until the account is seriously in the red. Beyond a certain threshold, say minus one thousand love units, the person feels the opposite of love, hate. The person feels incredibly repulsed by you whenever you are around.

You and the one you love certainly never want to feel that way about each other, but in many marriages spouses end up hating each other. They never intended to make each other miserable; it just turned out that way because they stopped making each other feel good and started making each other feel bad. Unexpectedly they not only fell out of love, but they actually began to hate each other.

When you were dating, you learned how to make each other happy and you did it so well that you fell in love with each other. You also learned how to avoid upsetting each other. So far, so good.

But will you keep it up for the rest of your married lives? If you do, you will have the marriage you both hoped for, and that feeling of love you have for each other will be with you for the rest of your lives.

Wedding Gifts That Guarantee a Lifetime of Love

This book is about wedding gifts—not just any wedding gifts—very special wedding gifts. They are gifts that will guarantee your love for the rest of your lives.

The wedding gifts that I recommend will encourage you to deposit love units into each other's Love Bank and discourage you from withdrawing them. By committing yourselves to the gifts, you will be following the guidelines you'd be using if you wanted to make someone love you.

Sadly, when a couple marry, they often stop doing what they did to create love for each other. They forget what it was that got them to the altar. But when you give the gifts of love to each other, you are continually reminded of how love is sustained and you guarantee that the feeling of love you now share will endure throughout your lives together.

When you learn what the four gifts are, you may think that any one of them would be sufficient to add love to your marriage. The truth is, however, that all four are necessary and interdependent. Unless you give each other all four gifts, the others will lose their value. After you learn about all four of the gifts, you will understand how each one complements the other three.

When you and your partner agree to give these four gifts to each other, complete the gift certificate in the front of this book. I guarantee you they will be the best gifts you will ever receive because they will sustain your love for the rest of your lives.

PART ONE

The Gift of Care

*I PROMISE TO MEET
YOUR MOST IMPORTANT
EMOTIONAL NEEDS*

Two

WHAT IS CARE?

What is care? That's a good question for a couple preparing for marriage. If in your wedding ceremony you promise to care for each other, you should know what that promise means.

Care is a word with many meanings in our language. When we say we care, it can mean that we are concerned about someone and hope that person will be happy in life. It can also mean that we have strong emotional feelings for a person. That's another way of saying that we love him or her.

However, I use the word *care* to mean what you *do* for each other, not how you *feel.* Care, to me, is your ability and willingness to meet each other's needs. When you promise to care for each other, you promise to do things

that will enhance the quality and enjoyment of each other's life.

You decided to marry because you have found each other irresistible and you simply can't live without each other. It's the Love Bank's fault. You managed to deposit so many love units into each other's Love Bank that you triggered the inevitable reaction of romantic love. That feeling of love has encouraged you to spend the rest of your lives together.

In fact it's your care that helped create your love. The way you have cared for each other has deposited huge sums of love units in your Love Bank. Do you know what you did to deposit so many love units into each other's Love Bank? Do you know what you will need to do to continue depositing them? In this section, I will explain how your care for each other deposits the love units that create and maintain your love for each other. I will show you how you managed to deposit all those love units and how you can keep them coming throughout your marriage.

Since the feeling of love has had so much to do with your decision to marry, you should fully understand how you got that feeling and what you can do to keep it. As I've already said, love is not a mystery, it's a predictable emotional reaction. The relationship between care and love is also predictable. Care can help create love. Lack of care can destroy it.

The Art of Caring

Some of us are naturally talented in making others feel good, but most of us have had to learn how to do it through trial and error. Fortunately as children we were usually quick to let each other know how we were being affected. When we did something others liked, they became our friends, and when we upset them, they became our enemies. But enemies could become friends and vice versa between recess and lunch. So as children we could redeem ourselves rather quickly if we had made a social blunder.

By the time we entered adolescence, most of us had figured out social etiquette well enough to have attracted friends who remained friends for weeks, or even months, at a time. Some of these friends were of the opposite sex, and that added a new dimension to the meaning of friendship.

We discovered that at least some of our opposite-sex friends gave us feelings that we had never felt before—better than any we had ever experienced. We were used to friends making us feel good, but this was ridiculous. Imagine, me, talking to some girl on the telephone for hours. I never did that with my best friend, Steve. Why did I do it with Joyce? Because it felt so good just to talk to her. And she apparently felt the same way talking to me. We were depositing love units into each other's Love Bank.

Just as I could make Joyce very happy, I could also upset her. I discovered that what worked well for my same-sex friends did not often find approval with my opposite-sex friends. Things that would never have bothered Steve, bothered Joyce. And I seemed to bother her almost effortlessly.

I played practical jokes on her that drove her nuts. My jokes withdrew all love units from my account in her Love Bank that had been deposited when we talked on the telephone.

But it isn't just someone making us feel good once in a while that creates romantic love in us. It is when someone does it continually and we feel sensationally good that we fall in love. There's a big difference between depositing a few love units and depositing carloads of them. So why waste our time with those who only deposit two or three love units, when we can be with someone who deposits hundreds? The most sought-after girls in my high school were those who knew how to make guys feel terrific every time they were together. Quite frankly, their appearance usually had a lot to do with it, but they also had other traits that boys found attractive.

In high school the boys that were most popular among the girls were those who knew how to make girls feel great, to sweep them off their feet. Those guys had learned the art of caring, the art of depositing love units. Those of us who were not among the most popular would often try to copy what we thought the popular boys were doing. Sometimes it worked and sometimes it didn't.

Care is definitely an art. You were artful enough to fall in love with each other. What did you do to deposit all those love units? What caused such a large deposit of love units to be made at one time that you broke through the love barrier and fell in love? It even took me a while to figure it out during my first few years as a marriage counselor. But eventually, through the help of hundreds of people I counseled, I discovered what it was. If your marriage is to be as successful as you hope it will be, you will need to discover it too. First, though, I should explain something that has a great deal to do with this—emotional needs.

What Is an Emotional Need?

We all know about physical needs, such as the need for food, water, oxygen, warmth, and so forth. These are essential to our survival, and with them our bodies thrive. Without them, we die.

There is also another kind of need that all of us have—emotional needs. When these needs are not met we don't die, but some of us wish we would. An emotional need is a craving that, when satisfied, leaves us feeling happy and content. When it's unsatisfied, we feel unhappy and frustrated.

Most physical needs are also emotional needs. Physical deprivation leads to emotional craving, and physical satisfaction leads to emotional contentment. Food is a good example. When we're hungry, a physical need for food is accompanied by an emotional craving for food. The same thing is true of water. But not every physical need is also an emotional need. For example, we need oxygen but we don't have an emotional reaction every time the need is not met. We can breathe, say, helium instead of oxygen and feel okay right up to the moment when we pass out. Oxygen is a physical need without an emotional component.

On the other hand, many emotional needs are not physical needs. What makes us feel good in life often has nothing to do with our physical well-being. In fact there are many emotional needs that, when met, actually threaten our physical health. For example, we put our health at risk when we yield to the emotional craving for drugs or alcohol.

There are probably thousands of emotional needs—a need for birthday parties (or at least birthday presents), peanut butter sandwiches, *Monday Night Football* . . . I could go on and on. Whenever one of our emotional needs is met, we feel good, and when it's not met, we feel bad. Try telling a football fan that he can't watch football this week, and you get a taste of how emotional needs affect people.

Not all emotional needs affect us with the same intensity. Some make us feel very good when met and very bad when unmet. Others have a very small effect on us. In other words, meeting some needs deposits many love units, while meeting others deposits only a few.

There are a few emotional needs that when met deposit so many love units that we fall in love with the person who meets them. These are the ones you met for each other during courtship, and you did such a good job meeting them that you fell in love.

Care Is Meeting the Most Important Emotional Needs

When you come right down to it, your agreement to care for each other is an agreement to meet each other's most important emotional needs. These are the needs that, when met, can make you fall in love with whoever meets them. That's why it's important for a couple to meet them for each other as exclusively as possible. When you let more than one person meet those emotional needs, you'll have fallen in love with too many people.

A couple give each other exclusive right to meet their emotional needs, so that they will love each other exclusively. This puts responsibility on their shoulders to see to it that the needs of the other are, in fact, met. After all, if your spouse promises not to let anyone else meet those needs, and then you fail to meet them, your spouse will be in a very unpleasant and frustrating situation. Sex is one of the more obvious exclusive emotional needs in marriage, but there are others that can be just as important to meet.

My counseling experience has helped me identify ten emotional needs so powerful that when met, they create romantic love. These ten emotional needs are affection, sexual fulfillment, conversation, recreational companionship, honesty and openness, physical attractiveness, financial support, domestic support, family commitment, and admiration. When these needs are met in marriage, people can experience great pleasure, and when they are not met, people experience great frustration and disappointment.

While almost everyone has these ten needs to some extent, people vary greatly in the way they are affected by them. For some, when the need for affection is met, a great deal of pleasure is felt; while for others, affection doesn't do much for them one way or another. The same can be said for admiration, some need it greatly, while others don't.

So while this list identifies the most common important emotional needs, all ten are not usually important for any one person. In fact I've found that, in general, only five out of the ten are identified by a person as important enough to create the feeling of romantic love when they are met. In other words, only five have the potential for depositing a great number of love units.

Since not all needs are equally important, it isn't necessary for a spouse to meet all ten needs in marriage. If a spouse simply learns to meet the five given highest priority, he or she will deposit enough love units to sustain romantic love. To a great extent, trying to meet the other needs would be a waste of time and energy.

Which of these needs are the five most important to the person you will marry? Which five are most important to you? It's very likely that the ones you pick will not be exactly the same as the ones your partner picks. In fact they may be entirely different.

One of the most important discoveries I made early in my counseling career was that men and women tend to prioritize these ten needs very differently.

Men tend to give highest priority to:

1. sexual fulfillment
2. recreational companionship
3. physical attractiveness
4. domestic support
5. admiration

These are the emotional needs that when met cause most men to fall in love with the woman who meets them. Women, on the other hand, tend to give the highest priority to:

1. affection
2. conversation
3. honesty and openness
4. financial support
5. family commitment

The men these women love usually meet these emotional needs for them. Of course not every man or woman has the same needs. Many men consider affection or conversation to be one of their top five needs, and many women rank admiration and sexual fulfillment among their most important needs. But on average, men and women rank these needs the way I listed them.

Since the way men and women tend to prioritize their needs is so different, it's no wonder they have difficulty adjusting in marriage! A man can set out to meet his wife's needs but he will fail miserably if he assumes that her needs are the same as his. A woman will also fail if she assumes her husband has the same needs as she has.

I have seen this simple error threaten many marriages. A husband and wife fail to meet each other's needs—not because they're selfish or uncaring, but because they are ignorant of what those needs are.

He may think he is doing her a big favor by inviting her to play golf with him (recreational companionship, a high-priority need for him), but she'll come home thoroughly frustrated because he didn't talk with her (conversation, one of her top needs). She hopes to please him by showering him with affection (which meets her need), but ends up frustrating him because her affection revs up his sexual engines (his need for sex), and she's not in the mood. Both partners think they are valiantly trying to meet the other's needs, but they are aiming at the wrong target.

Question: Where should you put your greatest effort so that you can deposit the most love units?
Answer: Meet each other's most important emotional needs.

Question: How can you discover which needs are the most important to each of you?
Answer: Ask.

As I've explained, you cannot assume that your spouse's needs will be the same as yours. You are the only one who can identify your most important emotional needs, and your partner is the best expert on his or her needs. You must ask if you want to know where to put your greatest effort. Before you ask, though, I'd like you to become familiar with the choices. Let's begin by taking a closer look at the ten emotional needs I listed. Then I'll explain how to decide which needs are the most important to meet, will deposit the most love units, and will demonstrate your care for each other.

Three

THE MOST IMPORTANT EMOTIONAL NEEDS

Do you know yourself well enough to list your most important emotional needs? Most people haven't given this much thought, and if forced to make up a list would not know where to begin. But it's very important that you understand your needs, not only for your own sake, but for the sake of your spouse. If he or she is going to put time and energy into becoming an expert at meeting those needs, you'd better be sure you've identified the right ones. And it's also important for you to understand your spouse's emotional needs so that you too can put your effort in the right place.

To help you identify your most important emotional needs, you will need the list of ten I have already given. But my list of needs may not include all of the needs that are most important to you. Ambition is a good example of a need that I have excluded from my list of ten needs. Some people gain tremendous pleasure from the ambition of their spouse. As long as their spouse continues to achieve important objectives, love units keep pouring in. But I found that need to be so uncommon that it did not make my final cut. In your case, however, it might make the cut, and you may want to include it as one of your most important emotional needs.

Needs such as ambition, that are not on my list of ten, should be included on your list if they are important to you. This will require you to identify them yourself, from your past experience. When you think about what makes you happiest, the times when these needs were met will come to mind.

For most of us, the ten needs that I listed cover the bases. I will describe each of them here, so you can determine which ones are most important to you. Remember, "craving" is an important ingredient in a need. If you have a craving for any of the following, it should be on your list.

Affection

Quite simply, affection is the expression of care. It symbolizes security, protection, comfort, and approval—vitally important ingredients in any relationship. When one spouse is affectionate to the other, the following messages are being sent:

You are important to me and I will care for you and protect you.
I'm concerned about the problems you face and will be there for you when you need me.

A simple hug can say those things. When we hug our friends and relatives, we are demonstrating our care for them. And there are other ways to show our affection. A greeting card, an "I love you" note, a bouquet of flowers, holding hands, walks after dinner, back rubs, phone calls, and conversations with thoughtful and loving expressions can all communicate affection.

Affection is, for many, the essential cement of a relationship. Without it, many people feel totally alienated. With it, they become emotionally bonded to the one showing the affection. If you feel terrific when the one you love is affectionate and you feel terrible when he or she isn't, you have the emotional need for affection.

Sexual Fulfillment

We often confuse sex and affection. This should help you sort them out: Affection is an act of love that is nonsexual and can be received from friends, relatives, children, and even pets with absolutely no sexual connotation. However, affectionate acts, such as hugging and kissing, done with a sexual motive are actually sex, not affection.

A sexual need usually predates your relationship with each other and is somewhat independent of your relationship. If you have always experienced a craving for sex, you have a sexual need. While you may have discovered a deep desire to make love to your future spouse since you've fallen in love, it isn't quite the same thing.

Sexual fantasies are usually a dead giveaway for a sexual need. If you have imagined what it would be like having your sexual need met in the most fulfilling ways, you probably have a sexual need. Incidentally, fantasies in general are good indicators of emotional needs. Whatever you fantasize the most about, usually reflects your emotional needs.

Because you have chosen each other as life partners, you will promise to be faithful to each other for life. This means that you will be each other's only sexual partner "until death do you part." You will make this commitment because you trust each other to meet your sexual needs, to be sexually available and responsive. The need for sex, then, is a very exclusive need, and if you have it, you will be very dependent on your spouse to meet it for you.

Conversation

Unlike sex, conversation is not an exclusive need. Our need for conversation can be ethically met by almost anyone. But if it is one of your most important emotional needs, whoever meets it best will deposit so many love units, you may fall in love with that person. So if it's your need, be sure that your partner is the one who meets it the best and most often.

If you see conversation as a practical necessity, primarily as a means to an end, you probably don't have much of a need for it. But if you have a craving just to talk to someone, if you pick up the telephone just because you feel like talking—to anyone—and enjoy conversation in its own right, consider it to be one of your most important emotional needs.

Men and women don't have too much difficulty talking to each other during courtship. That's a time of information gathering for both partners. Both are highly motivated to discover each other's likes and dislikes, personal background, current interests, and plans for the future.

But after marriage, many women find that the man who, before marriage, would spend hours talking to her, now seems to have lost all interest in talking and spends his spare time watching television or reading. If you have a craving for conversation, be sure to let your partner know about this need. That way, the great conversations you have shared during your courtship will continue throughout your marriage.

Recreational Companionship

A need for recreational companionship combines two needs into one. First, there is the need to be engaged in recreational activities and second, the need to have a companion. To determine if you have this need, first ask yourself if you have a craving for certain recreational activities. Then ask yourself if the activities require a companion for fulfillment. If the answer is yes to both questions, recreational companionship should be considered for your list.

During your courtship, you and your partner have probably been each other's favorite recreational companion. It's not uncommon for a woman to join a man in hunting, fishing, watching football, or other activities she would never have chosen on her own. She simply wants to spend as much time as possible with the man she likes, and that means going where he likes to go.

The same is true of a man. Shopping centers are no strangers to a man in love. He will also take his date out to dinner, watch romantic movies, and attend concerts and plays. A couple in love take whatever opportunity there is to be together and to be certain their partner wants more dates in the future.

I won't deny that marriage changes a relationship considerably. But does it have to bring an end to the activities that helped make the relationship so compatible? Can't a husband's favorite recreational companion be his wife, and vice versa? Think about it for a moment in terms of the Love Bank. How much do you enjoy these activities and how many love units would your spouse be depositing if you enjoyed them together? What a waste it would be if someone else got credit for all those love units! And if it were someone of the opposite sex, it would be downright dangerous! Who should get credit for all those love units? The one you should love the most, your spouse. That's precisely why I encourage couples to be each other's favorite recreational companion. It's one of the simplest ways to deposit love units.

If recreational activities are important to you, and someone must join you in them for them to be fulfilling, include recreational companionship on your list of needs.

Honesty and Openness

Most people want an honest relationship with their spouse. But some people have an emotional need for such a relationship. Honesty and openness give them a sense of security.

To feel secure, we want accurate information about our spouse's thoughts, feelings, habits, likes, dislikes, personal history, daily activities, and plans for the future. If a spouse does not provide honest and open communication, trust can be undermined and the feelings of security can eventually be destroyed. Then we can't trust the signals that are being sent and we have no foundation on which to build a solid relationship. Instead of adjusting, we feel off balance; instead of growing together, we grow apart.

Aside from the practical advantages of honesty and openness, you may find that you feel happy and fulfilled when your partner reveals his or her most private thoughts to you. You may also feel very frustrated when these thoughts are hidden. That reaction is evidence of an emotional need, one that can and should be met in marriage.

Physical Attractiveness

For many, physical attractiveness can be one of the greatest sources of love units. If you have this need, an attractive person will not only get your attention, but may distract you from whatever it was you were doing. In fact that's what may have first drawn you to your partner—his or her physical attractiveness.

There are some who consider this need to be temporary and important only at the beginning of a relationship. After a couple get to know each other better, some feel that physical attractiveness should take a back seat to deeper and more intimate needs.

But that's not been my experience, nor has it been the experience of many whom I've counseled, particularly men. For many individuals, the need for an attractive spouse continues on throughout marriage, and love units continue to be deposited whenever the spouse is seen.

Among the various aspects of physical attractiveness, weight generally gets the most attention. However, choice of clothing, hairstyle, makeup, and personal hygiene also come together to make a person attractive. Since attractiveness is usually in the eye of the beholder, you are the judge of what is attractive to you.

If the attractiveness of your partner makes you feel great, and loss of that attractiveness would make you feel very frustrated, you should probably include this need on your list.

Financial Support

People often marry for the financial security that their spouse provides them. In other words, part of the reason they marry is for money. Is financial support one of your important emotional needs?

It may be difficult for you to know how much you need financial support, especially before your marriage and if your partner has always been gainfully employed. But what if, before your marriage, your partner tells you not to expect any income from him or her. Would it affect your decision to marry? Or, what if after marriage your spouse cannot find work, and you have to financially support him or her throughout life? Would that withdraw love units?

What constitutes financial support? Earning enough to buy everything you could possibly desire or earning just enough to get by? Different people answer this differently, and the same person might answer differently in different stages of life. It is important to think about what your need is now and what it may be in the future. What would you expect in order to feel fulfilled? What would it take for you to feel frustrated?

Like many of these emotional needs, financial support is sometimes hard to talk about. As a result, many couples begin marriage with hidden expectations and assumptions. These can turn into resentment if they go unfulfilled.

You may have a need for financial support if you expect your spouse to earn a living and you definitely have that need if you do not expect to be earning a living yourself, at least during part of your marriage. Express this need clearly and you're more likely to have it fulfilled.

Domestic Support

The need for domestic support is a time bomb. At first it seems irrelevant, a throwback to more primitive times. But for many couples, the need explodes after a few years of marriage, surprising both of them.

Domestic support involves the creation of a peaceful and well-managed home environment. It includes cooking meals, washing dishes, washing and ironing clothes, housecleaning and child care. If you have the need for domestic support, you feel fulfilled when someone does these things for you and feel frustrated when you must do them yourself.

In earlier generations, it was assumed that all husbands had this need and all wives would naturally meet it. Times have changed, and emotional needs have changed along with them. Now many of the men I counsel would rather have their wives meet their needs for affection or conversation, needs that have traditionally been more characteristic of women. And many women, especially career women, gain a great deal of pleasure having their husbands create a peaceful and well-managed home environment.

Marriage usually begins with a willingness of both spouses to share domestic responsibilities. Newlyweds commonly wash dishes together, make the bed together, and divide many household tasks. The groom welcomes the help he gets from his wife with the chores he's been doing alone as a bachelor. At this point in marriage, neither of them would identify domestic support as an important emotional need. But the time bomb is ticking.

When does the need for domestic support explode? When the children arrive! Children create huge needs—both a greater need for income and more demanding domestic responsibilities. The previous division of labor becomes obsolete. Both spouses must take on new responsibilities—and which ones will they take?

Right now you may think you have no need for domestic support at all. But that may change later, and when it does, be ready to make up a new list of emotional needs. In fact, as soon as you expect to have your first child, you will find yourselves changing your priorities dramatically.

Family Commitment

In addition to a greater need for income and domestic responsibilities, the arrival of children creates in many people the need for family commitment.

Evidence of this need is a craving for your spouse's involvement in the educational and moral development of your children. When he or she helps care for them, you will feel very fulfilled, and when he or she doesn't, you will feel very frustrated.

Family commitment is not child care—feeding, clothing, or watching over children to keep them safe. Child care falls under the category of domestic support. Family commitment, on the other hand, is taking responsibility for the development of the children, teaching them your values so they will become successful adults.

As with domestic support, you may not have this need right now, because you don't have any children, but when children arrive, a change may take place that you didn't anticipate. And when it becomes an emotional need to you, be sure to communicate it to your spouse.

Admiration

If you have the need for admiration, some of the reason you fell in love with your partner may be that he or she compliments you. He or she may also be careful not to criticize you because criticism hurts you deeply.

Many of us have a deep desire to be respected, valued, and appreciated by the one we love. We need to be affirmed clearly and often. There's nothing wrong with feeling that way. Even God wants us to appreciate him.

The need for appreciation is one of the easiest needs to meet. Just a compliment or word of praise, and presto, you've just made somebody's day. On the other hand, it's also easy to be critical. A trivial word of rebuke can be very upsetting to people with this need, ruining their day and withdrawing love units at an alarming rate.

The person you plan to marry may have the power to build up or deplete his or her account in your Love Bank with just a few words. If words of praise or criticism easily affect you, be sure to add admiration to your list of important emotional needs.

Becoming an Expert

These ten emotional needs that I've just described are important to all of us. But only a few of the ten are so important to you that you fell in love with the person that met them, the person you plan to marry.

Most of our happiness in life comes from our relationships with others. That's because we can't meet our most important emotional needs by ourselves—others must meet them for us. And we usually fall in love with and marry the person we think will do the very best job meeting them. You have been each other's greatest source of happiness until now, and that should continue throughout your lives together.

Why don't more spouses try to become experts at meeting each other's emotional needs? Being an expert simply means that you have made an effort to learn what to do to make each other happy and you do it very well.

It's not really that difficult. In fact the secrets of a happy marriage are fairly easy to discover, if people would simply educate themselves. Marriage requires basic skills for success. People take courses regularly to become experts at all sorts of things—computer programming, business management, hairstyling. The wise couple will learn how to meet each other's emotional needs at expert level and throughout marriage will keep their skills finely tuned so that their marriage will be as fulfilling as possible for both spouses.

Four

IDENTIFYING AND MEETING IMPORTANT EMOTIONAL NEEDS

You and your partner want to care for each other. That's why you plan to marry: You want to care for each other for the rest of your lives. And, as I have already shown, you care for each other by meeting each other's most important emotional needs.

So now, I'll help you identify those needs. Then, to be sure that you follow through on your wedding vows, I will show you how you can guarantee each other that you'll meet those needs for the rest of your lives together.

What are your most important emo-tional needs? Only you can identify them. And your partner is the only one who can identify his or her needs.

Though I may know the emotional needs that most people have, I don't know the particular needs of an individual until that person tells me what they are.

It's difficult for most people to identify their needs without a lit-tle help. So in the last chapter, I introduced you to some of the most common emotional needs. From that list of ten needs, you were encouraged to select those that you know are important to you. If you haven't done so already, write down the needs you think are most important to you and ask your partner to do the same.

Remember, an emotional need is a craving that, when met, makes you feel happy and fulfilled, and when unmet makes you feel unhappy and frustrated. Try to determine what gives you the most pleasure when you have it, and what creates the most frustration when you don't have it. Add to your list needs you know you have that I didn't include in the last chapter. Try to think of everything you crave in life, and if there is something that is very important to your happiness, include it on the list. But when you do, try to define it as clearly as you can so that your partner will understand what it is.

After you have made a list of your most important emotional needs, rank them according to their priority for you. Imagine for a moment that your partner is willing to meet only one of the ten needs and is unwilling to meet any of the rest. If that were the case, which one of the ten emotional needs would you select?

Before you answer, consider this: If you don't choose sexual fulfillment as the most important need, you and your partner may never have sex together. If you don't choose affection, your partner may never hug or kiss you. If you don't choose financial support, your partner may not earn a dime throughout your life together. If your partner meets only one of the ten needs and the other nine are left unmet, which would give you the most satisfaction and the least frustration? Which would deposit the most love units? The need you select should be ranked number 1.

As you know, your marriage will not survive if only one of your needs is met. So if you were to be able to choose one more need from the list, remembering that all the others would be unmet by your spouse, which would you choose? That should be ranked number 2. Continue ranking your needs in order of their importance to you until you have chosen five. Each time you choose one, remember to consider all the others to be lost causes.

Before you leave this assignment, give your list of five needs one last look and give special attention to those you didn't include. If all five of the needs you've listed are met by your spouse, will you be happy? If your spouse fails to meet a need that is not included on your list, will it threaten to ruin your marriage? If there is a sixth need that either of you feels must be included to ensure the success of your marriage, add it to the list. But then let the other spouse also add a sixth need to his or her list.

My experience with most couples is that if they do an outstanding job meeting each other's top two emotional needs, that's all it takes to ensure romantic love. If couples do a reasonably good job meeting the other three, they add insurance to their marriage. But couples who try to meet all ten needs, try to do too much and usually do a poor or mediocre job on all of them. In those marriages, even though a great deal of effort is made, the results are very disappointing. But couples who focus their attention on the needs that mean the most, and ignore the rest, have sensational marriages.

So the needs you and your partner ranked number 1 and number 2 should get your very special attention. They are the ones you want to be experts in meeting for each other. If you leave them unmet in your marriage, your love for each other will be at risk. If someone outside the marriage meets them, he or she will become so attractive as to threaten your marriage. Affairs are usually caused when someone outside the marriage meets one of the two most important emotional needs.

Agree to Meet Each Other's Needs

When you and your partner have identified your five (or six) emotional needs, make a trade. You agree to meet your partner's emotional needs, and in return, your partner agrees to meet yours.

I suggest that you come to a formal understanding with each other. It's assumed that a husband and wife will care for each other, but because most marital agreements are so vague, they often fail to specify the care that is needed.

To help clarify your agreement, I have provided at the end of this book an Agreement to Meet the Most Important Emotional Needs for you and your partner to complete. There are spaces in the agreement for you to name the emotional needs you have identified as most important to each of you. After completing the agreement, sign it as an expression of your commitment to meet those needs for each other.

It would be wise to review your list every year, because needs change over time. Some years the change may not be very great, maybe just a reordering of needs. But in the year you have your first child, new needs may completely replace some of the old ones. That's when you must remind yourselves that care means meeting each other's most important emotional needs, even when those needs change during your lifetime together. And to know what they are, you will need to check with each other regularly.

Evaluate Your Effectiveness

Most people feel that they can meet their spouse's emotional needs if they simply know what they are. Affection, conversation, sexual fulfillment—these shouldn't be too difficult to manage. Besides, you are already doing a good job meeting many of each other's emotional needs, or you wouldn't be getting married. Why open a can of worms that, once opened, could ruin everything?

That's a good question, and it gets to the core of why many married couples don't try to evaluate each other's effectiveness unless the situation has deteriorated significantly. They often feel that it's insensitive to try to improve on their spouse's skills in meeting their needs.

It will be very tough for either of you to admit that an important need is not being met as it should be. For one thing, you are trying to be as supportive and encouraging to each other as possible. Criticism is exactly the opposite of what you want to express to each other. And yet, if you are dissatisfied with the way your partner is meeting your needs, it's important to reveal that fact now.

If you want to become skilled in anything, you must receive feedback as to how well you are doing. That way you are able to correct your mistakes and improve your overall performance. Learning to become an expert in meeting emotional needs also requires feedback. Otherwise, there is no way for you to know if you are effective in meeting them. Without feedback, your skills will suffer.

You have already identified your most important emotional needs, and that's an essential first step. By agreeing with each other to meet those needs, you have taken the second step. Now those needs represent your goals, and if you meet them, you will be providing the care that you expect in your marriage.

But how will you know if you are achieving those goals? How will you know if you are meeting the needs of your spouse? You should have a simple, yet sensitive, way to communicate your satisfaction or dissatisfaction with the way your important needs are being met.

Both you and your partner should answer the following questions about the most important emotional needs on your lists.

Are you satisfied with the way your partner is meeting this need?
If your answer is no, how would you like your partner to meet this need? Be specific.
Does your partner meet this need often enough?
If not, how often would you like your partner to meet this need? Be specific.

After you have carefully written your answers, show them to your partner. The feedback you both receive will help you determine if your skills are adequate or if they need improvement.

Improving Your Skills

Your partner's evaluation of how well you are meeting his or her needs considers two aspects of care—quality and quantity.

Quality is the way you go about meeting a need. For example, in meeting the need for conversation, you must learn how to make the conversation enjoyable for both you and your spouse. You simply cannot meet a need unless the quality of your care meets your spouse's minimum standard.

Quantity is how often and how long you spend meeting a need. Some people don't require fulfillment very often, while others want it frequently. Conversation is one of those needs that, for some, may be satisfied with a short chat, and for others, may be needed almost every waking moment.

When you learn to meet each other's emotional needs, you will need to satisfy both the quality and quantity requirements to make your partner happy. Quantity is fairly easy to understand, because your partner will tell you how often and how much he or she wants the need met.

But quality is more difficult to communicate. Sometimes even the one with the need doesn't understand exactly what's missing.

If you know that quality improvements are needed but you are at a loss to know how to make them, I suggest that you read *His Needs, Her Needs: Building an Affair-proof Marriage* and its accompanying workbook, *Five Steps to Romantic Love.* These books will help you think through each need and give you ideas as to how they can be met to each other's satisfaction.

Meet Each Other's Needs in Ways That Are Mutually Enjoyable

It turns out that there will be many effective ways to meet each other's emotional needs. Some of them will be enjoyable for you to follow, and others will be very unpleasant. Because you love each other so much, you will be tempted to meet each other's needs at all costs, even if it is unpleasant to do so. I strongly advise you to avoid this, however. You should have an understanding that you will try to meet each other's needs only in ways that are enjoyable for both of you. Never expect the other person to suffer or sacrifice so that your need can be met.

There is a great deal of wisdom behind this recommendation. The most important reason for avoiding sacrifice is that you care for each other, and that means neither of you wants the other one to suffer. How much gratification can you get knowing that your spouse is unhappy in the way he or she is meeting one of your needs? In fact most needs can be met only when your partner enjoys meeting them for you.

Take conversation, for example. If your partner is bored by a particular topic of conversation but knows that you like to talk about it for hours, how can you possibly be fulfilled by the conversation, knowing that he or she is very uncomfortable? The same is true for recreational companionship. Is it fun to engage in an activity with someone who would rather be somewhere else?

Sex is particularly sensitive to mutual enjoyment. If one spouse forces himself or herself into having sex as often as needed, does that make it fulfilling? I've counseled many wives who have agreed to have sex as often as requested, and their husband leaves every experience fuming. Why? Because she so obviously hated doing it with him. He would only be fulfilled if she enjoyed making love too.

So the skills you learn for meeting your partner's needs must take your own feelings into account. If you are to be a skilled conversationalist, you must pick topics that interest you as much as they interest your partner. Your recreational activities must be enjoyable to you as well as to him or her. And whenever you make love, the skills you develop must enable you to join your spouse in the sexual experience. Sacrifice in any area of needs fulfillment will not be satisfying to your partner.

There's another important reason for you to enjoy meeting your partner's needs and avoid sacrificing your own enjoyment: If you don't enjoy doing it, you won't be meeting the need very often. We tend to do what we enjoy the most and we avoid what we don't enjoy. The more you enjoy doing something, the more often you will do it. The less you enjoy something, the less you will do it. If your partner wants you to meet his or her need often, you must enjoy it a great deal.

A final reason for not sacrificing when meeting emotional needs is that it can create an aversive reaction. There are some spouses who are so disciplined that they can force themselves to sacrifice their feelings for an important cause. In marriage these people know that they are expected to meet certain needs but do not know how to enjoy meeting them. So they suffer whenever they try.

Sex is a good example of a need that these people try to meet by sacrificing their feelings. Whenever they make love, they suffer, but because they know it's required, they do it anyway. Such people often get headaches at the very thought of making love and use all sorts of lame excuses to get out of it. Eventually, after they have forced themselves to suffer long enough, they develop what psychologists call an aversion. It's a powerful negative emotional reaction that is conditioned to any unpleasant experience.

When an aversion to sex is developed, every sex act creates emotional symptoms that are overwhelmingly unpleasant. Eventually the pain is so great that sex must be abandoned entirely.

While most spouses never do experience such an aversive reaction, it's important to know that the risk can be avoided entirely by avoiding sacrifice. If you and your partner learn to meet each other's needs in ways that take each other's feelings into account, you will never experience the pain of an aversive reaction.

Don't ever think that your marriage can be built by sacrificing your own happiness. It is built only when you are both happy in the way you do things together. Personal sacrifice, however well intentioned it is, will undermine that mutual happiness. Neither of you wants the other to meet your needs reluctantly, and the only way to avoid that is to learn to meet them in ways that you both enjoy.

PART TWO

The Gift of Protection

*I PROMISE TO AVOID
BEING THE CAUSE
OF YOUR UNHAPPINESS*

Five

WHAT IS PROTECTION?

You love each other because you've done such a good job caring for each other—meeting each other's emotional needs. You have deposited so many love units in each other's Love Bank that you've exceeded the threshold necessary to experience the feeling of love.

But all those love units that you've carefully deposited during courtship can quickly be withdrawn in marriage. That's because once you're married, you can not only make each other very happy, but you can also make each other very unhappy.

Neither of you wants to hurt the other. Yet if you are not careful, you can become the greatest cause of each other's unhappi-

ness. And if you don't make a special effort to protect each other from yourselves, it's inevitable.

You may have already discovered how easy it is to hurt each other's feelings. And you have probably made a special effort to avoid being inconsiderate. You may have learned through experience to ask how the other person feels about something you're planning, just to be on the safe side.

Quite frankly, if you had not learned to be thoughtful, you probably wouldn't be marrying each other. Inconsiderate behavior withdraws so many love units that couples who indulge in such behavior don't stay in love very long. Your care for each other's needs created your love, but it's been your thoughtfulness that has kept your love alive. Will you continue to be as considerate after marriage?

To help you remember to be considerate of each other's feelings for the rest of your lives, I suggest that you give each other the second Gift of Love: protection. This gift provides protection from selfish tendencies that tempt you to gain at each other's expense, or worse yet, to deliberately try to hurt each other.

As a couple, almost everything you do affects each other, whether you want it to or not. Much of what you do makes your partner feel good. That's a very important reason for your choosing to marry each other. But you are also very capable of doing things that make the other person feel bad, and that's what the Gift of Protection will help you avoid.

Whenever you do something that makes your partner unhappy, you withdraw some love units. A single careless act is bad enough. But if you repeatedly do something that makes him or her unhappy, your Love Bank withdrawals can become serious enough to threaten your love for each other. I call behaviors that cause repeated withdrawals Love Busters, because they destroy romantic love.

In the simplest terms, Love Busters are those things you are likely to do on a regular basis that make your partner unhappy. They will rob enough love units from your account in your partner's Love Bank to destroy romantic love.

The Gift of Protection applies to any behavior that causes your partner unhappiness. But I focus special attention on Love Busters because, more than any other behavior in marriage, you'll need protection from them.

I have identified five categories of behavior that are Love Busters: angry outbursts, disrespectful judgments, annoying behavior, selfish demands, and dishonesty. Each category represents a type of thoughtless behavior that couples tend to repeat throughout their married life.

Why are we all tempted to do these things to each other? It's really quite easy to understand. While all of these habits may make others feel bad, for one reason or another, they tend to make us feel good. There is something in doing each of them that's in our own best interest. We do them because we like to do them. Love Busters give us comfort or pleasure, and we have a difficult time resisting them, even when we know we do them at our partner's expense.

Love Busters exist in most marriages, and you will need to take extraordinary precautions to avoid them in yours.

Angry Outbursts

What makes you angry? Anger usually occurs when you feel that (a) someone is making you unhappy, and (b) what they're doing just isn't fair. In your angry state, you're convinced that reasoning won't work, and the offender will keep upsetting you until he or she is taught a lesson. The only thing such people understand is punishment, you assume. Then they'll think twice about making you unhappy again!

Anger offers you a simple solution to your problem—destroy the troublemaker. If your partner turns out to be the troublemaker, your anger will urge you to hurt the one you've promised to cherish and protect. Anger does not care about his or her feelings and is willing to scorch the culprit if it helps even the score.

In the end, you have nothing to gain from anger. Punishment does not solve marital problems; it only makes your punished spouse want to inflict punishment on you. When you become angry with your spouse, you threaten your spouse's safety and security; you fail to provide protection. Your spouse may rise to the challenge and try to destroy you in retaliation. When anger wins, love loses.

Each of us has an arsenal of weapons we use when we're angry. If we think someone deserves to be punished, we unlock the gate and select an appropriate weapon. Sometimes the weapons are verbal (ridicule and sarcasm), sometimes they're devious plots to cause suffering, and sometimes they're physical. But they all have one thing in common: They are intended to hurt people. Since our partner is at such close range, we can use our weapons to hurt him or her the most.

Some of the husbands and wives I've counseled have fairly harmless arsenals, maybe just a few awkward efforts at ridicule. Others are armed to nuclear proportions, putting their spouse's life in danger. The more dangerous your weapons are, the more important it is to control your temper. If you've ever lost your temper in a way that has caused great pain and suffering to the one you love, you know you cannot afford to lose your temper again. You must go to extreme lengths to protect your partner from yourself.

Remember, in marriage you can be your spouse's greatest source of pleasure but you can also be your spouse's greatest source of pain, particularly when he or she receives the brunt of your anger.

Disrespectful Judgments

Have you ever tried to "straighten out" someone? We're all occasionally tempted to do it. We usually think we're doing that person a big favor, lifting him or her from the darkness of confusion into the light of our "superior perspective." If people would only follow our advice, we assume, they could avoid many of life's pitfalls.

But if you ever try to straighten out your spouse, to keep him or her from making mistakes, you are making a much bigger mistake. Your mistake withdraws love units and destroys romantic love. I call it disrespectful judgments.

A disrespectful judgment occurs whenever someone tries to impose a system of values and beliefs on someone else. When a husband tries to force his point of view on his wife, he's just asking for trouble. When a wife assumes that her own views are right and her husband is woefully misguided—and tells him so—she enters a minefield.

The trouble starts when you think you have the right—even the responsibility—to impose your view on your partner. Almost invariably, he or she will regard such imposition as personally threatening, arrogant, rude, and incredibly disrespectful. That's when you lose units in your Love Bank account.

When you try to impose your opinions on your partner, you imply that he or she has poor judgment. That's disrespectful. You may not say this in so many words, but it's the clear message that your partner hears. If you value your partner's judgment, you won't be so quick to discard his or her opinions. You will consider the possibility that your partner is right and you're wrong.

I'm not saying that you can't disagree with your partner. But you should *respectfully disagree*. Try to understand your partner's perspective. Present the information that brought you to your opinion and listen to the information he or she brings. Entertain the possibility of changing your mind, instead of just trying to change your partner's mind.

That's how respectful persuasion works. You see, each of us brings two things into a marriage—wisdom and foolishness. A marriage thrives when a husband and wife can blend their value systems, with each one's wisdom overriding the other's foolishness. By sharing their ideas, sorting through the pros and cons, a couple can create a belief system superior to what either partner had alone. But unless they approach the task with mutual respect—using respectful persuasion—the process won't work and they'll destroy their love for each other.

Annoying Behavior

When was the last time the person you are about to marry did something that annoyed you? Last week? Yesterday? An hour ago? Maybe your partner is humming that irritating tune this very minute!

One of the most annoying things about annoying behavior is that it doesn't seem all that important—but it still drives you bananas! It's not abuse or even disrespect, just annoyance. You should be able to shrug it off, but you can't. It's like the steady drip, drip of water torture. Annoying behavior will nickel and dime your Love Bank into bankruptcy.

When we're annoyed, others seem inconsiderate, particularly when we've explained that their behavior bothers us and they continue to do it. It's not just the behavior itself, but the thought behind it—the idea that they don't care.

But when our behavior annoys others, we have an entirely different perspective. *It's just a little thing; why make a federal case out of it? Why can't other people adjust?*

I hear married couples say things like:

"If Sam loved me, he'd let our cats sleep with us at night."

"If Ellen were not so self-centered, she'd encourage me to go bowling with my friends every Thursday."

As a counselor, I try to help couples become more empathetic, to see through each other's eyes. Of course, no one can fully imagine what someone else feels, and that's a great part of the problem. I often wish I could switch a couple's minds: Sam becomes Ellen for a day and Ellen becomes Sam. If they could only know what it feels like to experience their own insensitive behavior, they would change their ways in a hurry.

I've found it helpful to divide annoying behavior into two categories. If behavior is repeated without much thought, I call it an *annoying habit*. If it's usually scheduled and requires thought to complete, I call it an *annoying activity*. Annoying habits include personal mannerisms, such as the way you eat, the way you clean up after yourself (or don't!), and the way you talk. Annoying activities include sporting events you attend, your choice of church, or your personal exercise program.

Every annoying habit or activity will drive a wedge between you and your partner, creating and sustaining incompatibility. If you want compatibility in your marriage, and you want to avoid squandering love units, get rid of that annoying behavior now!

Selfish Demands

Our parents made demands on us when we were children; teachers made demands in school; and employers make demands at work. Most of us didn't like them as children and we still don't.

Demands carry a threat of punishment. If you refuse me, you'll regret it. In other words, you may dislike doing what I want but if you don't do it, I'll see to it that you suffer even greater pain. In the Godfather's terms, a demand is "an offer you can't refuse."

People who make demands don't seem to care how others feel. They think only of their own needs. If you find it unpleasant to do what I want, tough! And if you refuse, I'll make it even tougher.

Demands depend on power. They don't work unless the demanding one has the power to make good on his threats. The Godfather had the power to make those "unrefusable" offers. A four-year-old who demands a new toy does not have that power—unless you count the ability to embarrass you by screaming bloody murder in the middle of a crowded store.

Ideally in a marriage, there is shared power—the husband and wife working together to accomplish mutual objectives with mutual agreement. But when one spouse starts making demands—along with threats that are at least implied—power is no longer shared. As a result, the threatened spouse often strikes back, fighting fire with fire, power with power. Suddenly the marriage is a tug of war instead of a bicycle built for two. It's a test of strength—who has enough power to win? When one spouse wins and the other loses, the marriage loses.

Demands are the wrong way to get what you need from each other. When you ask your partner to do something for you, he or she may cheerfully agree to it or may express reluctance. This reluctance may be due to any number of causes—personal needs, comfort level, a sense of what's wise or fair. But be assured that there is a reason for reluctance, and from your partner's viewpoint, it's a good reason.

If after your partner expresses reluctance you insist on your request, making it a demand, what are you doing? You are declaring that your wishes are more important than his or her feelings. And you are threatening a distressful outcome if your demands are not met.

Now your partner must choose the lesser of two evils—your "punishment" on the one hand or his or her cause for reluctance on the other. Your partner may ultimately submit to your demand, but you will withdraw love units in the process. You may get your way but you will do so at his or her expense. I guarantee you, your spouse will feel used, and rightfully so.

Sometimes a wife says, "But you don't know my husband! He lies around the house all night and I can't get him to do a thing. The only time he lifts a finger is to press the remote control. If I don't demand that he get up and help me, nothing would get done."

"Requests don't work with my wife," a husband might say. "She only thinks about herself! She spends her whole life shopping and going out with her girlfriends. If I didn't demand that she stay at home once in a while, I'd never see her."

My answer is that demands are an ineffective way to get a husband to help around the house or keep a wife from going out with her friends. Demands do not encourage people to cooperate; they only withdraw love units. If you force your spouse to meet your needs, it becomes a temporary solution at best, and resentment is sure to rear its ugly head. Threats, lectures, and other forms of manipulation do not build compatibility. They build resentment.

Dishonesty

Dishonesty is the strangest of the five Love Busters. No one likes dishonesty, but sometimes honesty seems more damaging. What if the truth is more painful than a lie?

When a wife first learns that her husband has been unfaithful, the pain is often so great that she wishes she had been left ignorant. When a husband discovers his wife's affair, it's like a knife in his heart—maybe it would have been better not knowing, he thinks. In fact many marriage counselors advise clients to avoid telling a spouse about past infidelity, because it's too painful for people to handle. Besides, if it's over and done with, why dredge up the sewage of the past?

It's this sort of advice that leads some of the most well-intentioned husbands and wives to lie to each other, or at least give each other false impressions. They feel that dishonesty will help them protect each other's feelings.

This makes dishonesty a strange Love Buster. Lies clearly hurt a relationship over the long term, but truth can also hurt, especially in the short term. That's why many couples continue in dishonesty—because they feel they can't take the shock of facing the truth, at least right now. As a result, the marriage dies a slow death.

Honesty is like a flu shot. It may give you a short, sharp pain but it keeps you healthier over the following months.

I draw a distinction between the pain of a thoughtless act and the pain of *knowing* about a thoughtless act. Honesty sometimes creates some pain, the pain of knowing. But it is really the thoughtless act itself that causes the pain, not the honesty. Dishonesty may defer some of that pain but, more likely, it compounds the pain. When the truth is finally revealed, the months or years of hiding it make everything worse.

Dishonesty strangles compatibility. To create and sustain compatibility, you must lay your cards on the table; you must be honest about your thoughts, feelings, habits, likes, dislikes, personal history, daily activities, and plans for the future. When misinformation is part of the mix, you have little hope of making successful adjustments to each other. Dishonesty not only makes solutions to problems hard to find, but it often leaves couples ignorant of the problems themselves.

There's another very important reason to be honest. Honesty makes our behavior more thoughtful. If we knew that everything we did and said would be televised and reviewed by all our friends, we would be far less likely to engage in thoughtless acts. Criminals would not steal and commit violent acts if they knew they would be caught each time they did. Honesty is the television camera in our lives. If we are going to be honest about all that we do, revealing everything to others, we tend not to engage in thoughtless acts because we know those acts will be revealed—by ourselves.

In an honest relationship, thoughtless acts are revealed, forgiven, and corrected. Bad habits are nipped in the bud. Honesty keeps a couple from drifting into incompatibility. As incompatible attitudes and behaviors are revealed, they can quickly become targets for elimination. But if these attitudes and behavior remain hidden, they are left to grow out of control.

Keeping Love Busters out of Your Marriage

So, there they are, five Love Busters that will destroy your love for each other—unless you do something to keep them out of your marriage. You are planning to marry each other because, up to now, you have done such a good job caring for each other. But if after you marry you allow any of these Love Busters to gain a foothold and grow, all the care in the world will not save your marriage.

The second Gift of Love, protection, will keep your love for each other secure. When you protect each other from Love Busters, you will grow in love and compatibility. If you fail to protect, you will grow apart.

After reading about the five Love Busters, you may be wondering if there is a simple way to remind yourselves to avoid them. There is, and it's the topic of the next chapter. I call it the Policy of Joint Agreement. If you follow this Policy, you will prevent Love Busters from taking root and growing in your marriage.

Six

THE POLICY
OF JOINT AGREEMENT

Love Busters will always stand in the way of your marital happiness. If you allow these habits to grow, you will become very unhappy and your marriage may not last very long. Angry outbursts, disrespectful judgments, selfish demands, annoying behavior, and dishonesty—they are all dangerous habits.

Your Gift of Protection will help guard you against these Love Busters. By agreeing not to be the cause of each other's unhappiness, it will be much easier for you to identify Love Busters whenever they show their ugly faces. That's because you now know that whenever

you're angry, disrespectful, demanding, annoying, or dishonest, you are hurting your spouse—something you have promised to avoid.

But by the time you identify a Love Buster, it's too late. You have already broken your promise. Some damage has already been done. True, you can set damage control into action by apologizing and trying to avoid the harmful act in the future. But isn't there a way to avoid Love Busters *before* they appear?

With the goal of the total elimination of Love Busters, I've written a Policy to help you implement the Gift of Protection. This Policy will not only help you avoid Love Busters, but it will help create a lifestyle that will protect your partner.

This policy will protect you from each other's self-centeredness. It is especially valuable when you don't feel like following it. If you make all of your decisions together, and avoid final choices until there is an enthusiastic agreement, you build a partnership that will last for life.

The Policy of Joint Agreement

Never do anything without an enthusiastic agreement between you and your spouse.

The reason that the Policy of Joint Agreement protects you so well is that it forces you to take each other's feelings into account with every decision you make. This means that you won't subject your partner to your anger, disrespect, annoying behavior, demands, or dishonesty because there's no way your spouse would be enthusiastic about this behavior. You have probably already been following the policy, without ever being told what it is. If so, it explains why you feel so safe with each other.

But after marriage both of you will be tempted to make decisions that are not acceptable to the other, and when you are tempted, the Policy of Joint Agreement should be there to prevent you from making a disastrous mistake—gaining at each other's expense.

Creating a Compatible Lifestyle

Building your life together is like building a house—brick by brick. Each brick is a choice you make about the way you live together. If you follow the Policy of Joint Agreement and make choices that are mutually agreeable, your house will be strong and beautiful. But if some bricks are acceptable to only one of you, those weak bricks will make your whole house an uncomfortable place to live.

Compatibility means that you live in harmony with each other. It means enjoying the lifestyle you created because it is what both of you want and need. Each brick that goes into your house is there because you are both comfortable with it.

Incompatibility, on the other hand, is created when the Policy of Joint Agreement is not followed, when one partner adds bricks that may be in his or her own best interest but are not in the other's best interest. All acts of self-interest, at the other's expense, not only withdraw love units, but also undermine the very fabric of marriage—safety and trust. Incompatibility, therefore, is simply the accumulation of thoughtless habits and activities. The more of them a couple try to tolerate, the more incompatible they become.

Most marriages start off with very few thoughtless habits because successful courting usually gets rid of them. Couples who are considering marriage try hard to behave thoughtfully because if they don't, they won't get to the altar.

But after marriage, thoughtless behaviors usually begin to appear. In the name of personal freedom, private interests, and expanding horizons, spouses develop habits and activities that do not take each other's feelings into account. Before long, they are no longer compatible.

An extreme but common example of what happens when a couple become incompatible is an affair. People have an affair because it meets their emotional needs and makes them feel good. The fact that the affair hurts their spouse does not deter them. An affair creates instant incompatibility because as long as it's tolerated, there's no way that a couple can live together in harmony. It's a brick that threatens to destroy the entire house.

You may be uncomfortable with my example, because you assume that an affair could never happen to your marriage. But it happens in over 50 percent of marriages and it is the most common complaint I hear from couples I counsel. Most of the offended spouses are grief stricken when they find out about an affair. They never thought it would happen to them.

But infidelity does not come as an isolated failure to follow the Policy of Joint Agreement in these marriages. It's only one of many decisions both spouses made that failed to take each other's feelings into account. In fact spouses in these marriages are usually in the habit of *not* taking each other's feelings into account. They build marriages in which they make independent decisions that create independent lifestyles. Their independence often leads to romantic relationships and lovers outside of their marriage.

The bottom line is that couples need to eliminate behavior that is good for one and bad for the other, even if it makes the one eliminating it feel bad at first. In the long run, the gains from having a mutually agreeable lifestyle more than outweigh the loss of an independent lifestyle. But thoughtless behavior is not easy to avoid. Most people feel resentful if they must give up something they enjoy, even if it makes the one they love unhappy.

Giving Up Thoughtless Behavior

How should you deal with the resentment of having to give up thoughtless behavior? At this point in your relationship, this may seem like a strange question to ask. Resentment about giving up thoughtless behavior? How could either of you become resentful about giving up something that would hurt the other? The question may seem strange now, but I guarantee you, there will be a point in your marriage when it will be precisely what you will be asking yourself. So in anticipation of that question, I'll try to give you the answer.

There are two kinds of resentment: (1) resentment due to something your spouse *did* to you that was hurtful, and (2) resentment due to *not doing* something you would like to do because it would hurt your spouse. The first kind of resentment comes from an action that intentionally hurts the other person, while the second kind of resentment simply comes from inaction. Resentment caused by a spouse's thoughtless behavior is usually much greater than resentment caused by missing out on something.

To illustrate, I will use the experiences of Kathy and John.

Kathy had an opportunity to attend an office party but she knew that her husband, John, would not want her to go without him. Since spouses were not invited, and she wanted to go, she simply went to the party alone. She let him know about her plans by leaving a message on the answering machine.

John experienced the first kind of resentment. Kathy chose to do something that made her feel good but made her husband feel bad. She justified it as something she had to do for herself. Marriage, she reasoned, was not slavery, and John had no right trying to control her behavior.

But John would not have tried to control her behavior. If she had asked him how he felt about her decision, he would have told her that he did not like it. That's not an effort to control, that's simply the honest expression of an emotional reaction.

What made John resentful was that Kathy did something that hurt him. When she finally arrived home at 4:00 A.M., he was still awake and was an emotional wreck. Kathy argued that he could feel any way he wanted to feel and that he was upset because he chose to be upset, not because she had done anything to upset him.

There was nothing John could do to convince Kathy that it was her thoughtless behavior that upset him. He concluded that she did not care about how he felt, and that made him even more resentful.

Let's imagine a different scenario for this couple. Suppose Kathy asked John how he would feel being left alone while she went to the office party. And suppose John told her that it was unacceptable to him. Then if Kathy decided not to go to the party, she would be vulnerable to the second kind of resentment. She would be resentful for having to give up a good time just because John didn't approve. She may have thought, "He doesn't care enough about me to want me to have fun."

If you follow the Policy of Joint Agreement, you guarantee avoiding the first kind of resentment but you risk experiencing the second kind.

In our first scenario, Kathy chose not to have the second kind of resentment. She decided to please herself and go to the party. It was only John who would suffer resentment—the first kind—because of Kathy's selfish decision.

But if Kathy had seen her marriage to John as a partnership where decisions should not be made if either spouse suffers, then Kathy would have negotiated with John in the hope of arriving at an alternative that they could both accept. If they didn't come up with an alternative by the time the party began, she risked the second kind of resentment.

Couples that learn to follow the Policy of Joint Agreement, however, develop such skill in negotiating with each other that mutually acceptable alternatives are the rule. For these couples the second kind of resentment is the exception.

John had a great deal of trouble recovering from Kathy's night out because her thoughtlessness struck at the very core of their relationship. Her decision proved to him that his feelings were not important to her.

But what about Kathy's feelings? If John cared about Kathy, wouldn't he have sacrificed his own feelings so that she could have a good time?

That brings up a dangerous practice: sacrificing for each other. Suppose Kathy had asked John how he felt about her attending the party alone, and he said he wanted her to go so that she could enjoy herself. Isn't sacrifice a sign of love? Isn't that what caring spouses should do for each other?

Not if they follow the Policy of Joint Agreement. "How would you feel?" is the question, not, "Do I have your permission?" John was very uncomfortable about her going to the party alone. If he expressed his feelings honestly, he could not "enthusiastically" agree to her going.

Mutual love dictated that John and Kathy had to make a decision that satisfied both of their needs simultaneously. And since self-centered thinking gets in the way of love every once in a while, they needed the Policy of Joint Agreement to make a mutually caring decision.

John and Kathy had to learn to behave in ways that did not hurt each other. In this case, Kathy could not go to the party because doing so would hurt John. They had to learn to create a lifestyle that was enjoyable for both of them. But that didn't mean they would be burdened with disappointments. It didn't mean they would spend the rest of their lives in a closet. It meant they had to become creative in making choices that would lead to mutual happiness.

I suggested to Kathy that she write a letter to her company explaining that she would not be able to attend future office parties unless her husband were invited. The company changed their policy regarding spouses' attendance, and from then on, both she and John attended the parties together.

Sometimes solutions are not that simple. But even difficult solutions are worth the effort it takes to come up with them. Couples should not waste time on choices that make only one of them happy.

The Policy of Joint Agreement may make you uncomfortable once in a while. Until you arrive at a mutually enjoyable way of living, you may need to stop by the side of the road and plan which fork in the road you will be taking together. That means at times you will not be moving forward at all, and it may be momentarily frustrating not to be making progress. But it's far better to look at the map and decide which road is the correct one than to take the wrong route just to be going somewhere.

How to Negotiate with the Policy of Joint Agreement

Whenever you and your spouse cannot agree on a decision, there is a procedure that I recommend. It will help you get into the habit of following the Policy of Joint Agreement.

1. *Set ground rules to make negotiations pleasant and safe.* Before you start to negotiate, agree with each other that you will both follow these rules: (a) be pleasant and cheerful throughout your discussion of the issue; (b) put safety first—do not threaten to cause pain or suffering when you negotiate, even if your negotiations fail; and (c) if you reach an impasse, stop for a while and come back to the issue later. Under no circumstances should you be disrespectful or judgmental of each other's opinions or desires. Your negotiations should accept and respect your differences. Otherwise, you will fail to make them pleasant and safe.

2. *Identify the problem from the perspectives of both you and your spouse.* Be able to state each other's position on the issue before you go on to find a solution. Each of you should describe what you would like and why you would like it. Then explain the other's position to each other's satisfaction. Be sure you fully understand each other before you go any further toward an agreement. And respect your differences of opinion.

3. *Brainstorm solutions with abandon.* Spend some time thinking of all sorts of ways to handle the problem and don't correct each other when you hear of a plan that you don't like—you'll have a chance to do that when you come to the fourth step. If you use your imagination, you will have a long list of possible solutions.

4. *Choose the solution that is appealing to both of you.* From your list of solutions, some will satisfy only one of you but not both. However, scattered within the list will be solutions that both of you find attractive. Among those solutions that are mutually satisfactory, select the one that you both like the most. But if you can't find one that you both agree to enthusiastically, go back to step 3 and brainstorm some more.

Remember, every time you try to force your partner into a way of life that is unpleasant, you are chipping away at his or her love for you. Not only is it a thoughtless way to accomplish your objectives, but it also won't get the job done. Sooner or later your partner will figure out a way of escaping you and your unpleasant way of life. A far better way to accomplish the same objectives is to find a way that takes your partner's feelings into account. That will build your love for each other.

The Policy of Joint Agreement will help your decisions stand up to the test of time. They will be decisions that will provide a strong foundation for your life together. The

Policy will also help you share power with each other. With it, neither of you will be a slave or a master. And you won't feel alone or abandoned in your effort to achieve your important objectives. You will become each other's willing partner in building a life of love and care.

Create a Compatible Lifestyle with the Gift of Protection

Your lifestyle is the accumulation of all of your habits and activities that make up the life you live. Until now, each of you created your own individual lifestyle that made you happy. You chose your job, your car, your residence, and you even chose each other because it's what each of you wanted individually.

But as soon as you marry, your lifestyle will change. Every day you will make decisions that will form a new lifestyle—your married lifestyle. With each decision, new habits and activities will begin to take shape. They will form the framework for a structure that will be in the process of completion for years to come. If you are not careful, though, you may create a lifestyle that may work for one of you and drive the other crazy.

Now is the time to realize that your new lifestyle must be created with mutual consideration. The lifestyle you choose must be carefully selected to make not just one of you, but both of you, very happy. That's why its creation must be guided by the Gift of Protection. With this special gift, you will protect each other from your self-centeredness whenever you make a decision.

If you would like help in learning to create a compatible lifestyle, read *Give and Take: The Secret to Marital Compatibility.* I wrote that book to help couples follow the Policy of Joint Agreement with every decision they make. Another book that can help you create a compatible lifestyle is *Your Love and Marriage: Dr. Harley Answers Your Most Personal Questions.*

Does Complaining Violate the Gift of Protection?

The lifestyle you and your partner create in marriage for each other will require many adjustments. A plan that both of you once thought would be great may turn out to be not so great, at least for one of you. When that happens, complaining usually begins.

A complaint is nothing more than feedback that your lifestyle needs further adjustment. You may hear a complaint regarding an emotional need that is not being met or about a Love Buster that has crept into your life. Whatever the complaint is, it reflects the need for a change, a change that will accommodate the spouse who's complaining.

But complaining can be a real show stopper. If you want to withdraw love units in a hurry, try complaining for a while. Well, then, isn't complaining a Love Buster?

Complaining itself isn't a Love Buster, but complaints often accompany Love Busters. If anger, disrespect, or demands become a part of your innocent request for change, then your complaint becomes a Love Buster. But what if your complaint simply takes the form of a request for change? Then, even though your spouse may feel uncomfortable knowing that there's work ahead, it's not a Love Buster. It falls into the category of honesty.

To hear a complaint for the first time does not usually withdraw many love units. It's when the complaint is repeated in almost every subsequent conversation that it becomes tedious. If you learn to address each complaint with a plan of action as soon as the complaint is raised, you greatly reduce the risk of the complaint being repeated.

If you and your partner go into your marriage with a willingness to deal with complaints as soon as they arise, respectfully and pleasantly, they will never overwhelm you. It's only when you let them pile up from years of neglect that you finally feel overwhelmed.

I have shown you how to negotiate with the Policy of Joint Agreement. If you learn to handle all of your complaints with this method, you will find yourselves eliminating your problems just about as fast as they arrive. And you will do it with protection, without hurting each other.

Seven

IDENTIFYING AND OVERCOMING LOVE BUSTERS

Wouldn't it be great if you never hurt each other throughout your marriage? Or if when one of you hurt the other by mistake, you would immediately apologize and take steps to avoid doing it again?

If you follow the Policy of Joint Agreement right from the beginning of your marriage, that's how your marriage will turn out— your love for each other will be guarded by mutual protection.

The failure to protect your spouse is a greater disaster in marriage than the failure to care. This is largely due to the fact that once you unleash pain on your partner, his or her desire to meet your needs evaporates.

There's no point in discussing emotional needs as long as Love Busters dominate a relationship, because when a person is in pain he or she doesn't want to meet needs or even have needs met.

That's why a willingness to care is often negated by an unwillingness to protect. Many couples who come to me for counseling have stopped caring for each other because Love Busters have made care disappear. Love Busters not only withdraw love units that were deposited by meeting emotional needs, but they also prevent more love units from being deposited, because they stop care right in its tracks. It's of critical importance to root out Love Busters if you want to keep your Love Bank balances high.

Love Busters don't belong in your marriage. Whatever excuse you may have to tolerate them, it can never justify the damage they do. Angry outbursts, disrespectful judgments, annoying behavior, selfish demands, dishonesty—every one of them will hurt your love for each other because they hurt you.

Love Busters usually don't enter a relationship with a full-scale invasion. They often begin with a seemingly harmless foothold. But from this inauspicious beginning, they grow to become ugly, destructive habits that can ruin your marriage.

If you have already allowed Love Busters to gain a foothold, they probably have not yet developed to maturity, or you would not be planning to marry each other. But if you don't get rid of them now, they may ruin any hope of a lifetime of love together.

So I suggest that you follow this four-step plan to help you identify and eliminate any Love Busters that may have nosed their way into your relationship. If you find any Love Busters, this plan will help you eliminate them quickly so they don't grow to do serious damage.

Step 1: Identify Love Busters

Before you go to battle, you need to know your enemy. And if you're battling Love Busters, you need to know what they are and how they express themselves. I have identified five broad types of Love Busters that can turn us all into monsters, but which of these are especially threatening to your relationship, and what specific behavior is involved?

One partner is often ignorant of the things he or she does to hurt the other. Love Busters can become second nature, habits we don't even think about. The perpetrator often doesn't even remember doing them. That's why the person on the receiving end of these Love Busters has to identify them, because that person is the one who feels the pain. You must tell each other what makes you unhappy.

To do this, review the five categories of Love Busters given in chapter 5. Consider whether each type is present in your relationship. If your partner indulges in one or more Love Busters, write it down. For each one, write down how often it occurs, the form it takes, the form it takes that hurts you the most, when the behavior started, and how it has developed. Your partner should make a list as well, and after both lists are complete, give them to each other to review.

None of us likes to be criticized, and when we are, we often react defensively. If you're not careful, you may respond to your spouse's revelations with anger and disrespect, those very Love Busters you are trying to eliminate. This is especially true if angry outbursts and disrespectful judgments are Love Busters that need your special attention.

So when you read each other's list, be careful to accept the evaluation with the Gift of Protection in mind. You have promised to protect each other, and your lists will help you discover areas of weakness. You may feel hurt by what you read, but an honest assessment of your conduct is not a violation of the Policy of Joint Agreement or the Gift of Protection. It is simply information you ask each other to provide that will help you do a better job of protecting each other.

Step 2: Identify Love Busters That Cause the Greatest Pain

In some marriages, all five types of Love Busters are ruining the relationship. But for most, it's only two or three that cause most of the problems. Whether all five are present, or only two, the partners should begin by focusing most of their attention on the one that's the worst. Once they have a handle on it, they can then turn to the next most troublesome Love Buster.

To help you choose which Love Buster should be tackled first, you need to rank the Love Busters in terms of their impact on your relationship. Decide which Love Buster causes you the greatest unhappiness and rank that 1. Continue ranking the Love Busters on your list until you have ranked them all.

I suggest that you focus your attention on only one or possibly two Love Busters at a time. But if there are others that are seriously affecting your relationship, they may require attention as well.

Step 3: Agree to Eliminate Love Busters for Each Other

It's easy for you to understand why your partner should change to protect you, but it's usually more difficult to understand why you should change to protect him or her.

However, if you have given each other the Gift of Protection, it's essential that you believe each other's assertion that changes are necessary.

As a concrete act of protection, I suggest that you make a commitment to eliminate the Love Busters that your spouse has identified. To help you formalize your intentions, you'll find an Agreement to Overcome Love Busters at the end of this book. It provides a space for you and your partner to list the Love Busters you will eliminate for each other's protection.

Step 4: Overcome the Love Busters

You know what you need to do, now do it!

Since you are just beginning your marriage, it can be that easy. You have not yet had enough time for your bad habits to be deeply imprinted, so you should be able to eliminate them quickly. You may find that it's simply a matter of agreeing to do it. Once you've decided to do it, you may find that you never indulge in the bad habits again.

But for some couples, it isn't quite that simple. They need a plan to follow and someone to hold them accountable to complete the plan. If you find that you continue to hurt your partner after you have made a reasonable effort to overcome Love Busters, you may need outside help.

Marriage support groups sponsored by churches or community organizations enable couples to overcome Love Busters by being accountable to others in the group. The group will check up on you, holding you to your promises.

Or you may want to ask a marriage counselor to hold you accountable. They are trained to monitor your progress and remind you of your commitment. You cannot afford to spend much time trying to overcome Love Busters, because they do so much damage. If your relationship is to survive, you must root them out quickly. If one counselor or method doesn't seem to be helping you do that, find another.

If you would like to read more on this subject, I suggest *Love Busters: Overcoming Habits That Destroy Romantic Love*. Its accompanying workbook, *Five Steps to Romantic Love*, contains worksheets to help you create an effective plan to keep those rascals from ruining your marriage.

PART THREE

The Gift of Honesty

*I PROMISE TO BE
HONEST WITH YOU*

Eight

WHAT IS HONESTY?

I addressed the subject of honesty when I introduced you to the first and second Gifts of Love. The first Gift of Love, care, was a promise to meet each other's most important emotional needs. If you or your partner selected honesty and openness as an important need that should be met in your marriage, you will be honest as a way of caring for each other.

Then when you gave each other the second Gift of Love, protection, you promised not to be the cause of each other's unhappiness. One of the Love Busters that causes emotional pain is dishonesty. So you will be honest as a way of protecting each other.

Since we have already discussed this topic of honesty twice, you may wonder why I bring it up again.

I introduce honesty as the third Gift of Love, because it has a unique purpose in marriage. Honesty is more than an emotional need that must be met to sustain love and more than a way to avoid unhappiness. Honesty is the only way that you and your spouse will ever come to understand each other. Without honesty, the adjustments that are crucial to the creation of compatibility in your marriage will never be made. Without honesty, your best efforts to resolve conflicts will be wasted because you will not understand each other well enough to find mutually acceptable solutions.

Honesty Helps You Aim at the Right Target

Most couples do their best to make each other happy—but their efforts, however sincere, are often misdirected. They aim at the wrong target.

Imagine a man who buys his wife flowers every night on the way home from work. What a wonderful thing to do—except his wife is allergic to them. Because she appreciates the gesture, she never mentions her allergies, but just sniffles in silence. Soon, however, she begins to dread the thought of her husband coming home with those terrible flowers. Meanwhile, he's getting bored with the marriage because she is always feeling lousy and never has energy to do anything—because of her allergies. But of course he won't tell her that.

Their marriage is in trouble, not because of any lack of effort, but because of their ignorance—ignorance caused by a lack of honesty. He thinks he's making her happy by bringing home flowers, but he doesn't realize that's the cause of their malaise. Let's say that, in his effort to show even more love for her, he brings home more and more flowers. Ultimately she collapses on the couch, gasping for breath, surrounded by flowers, while he wonders why she doesn't seem to appreciate his kindness.

It's a preposterous story but it portrays the way many couples misfire in their attempts to please each other. Their lack of honesty keeps them from correcting their real problems. Husbands and wives often misinform each other about their feelings, activities, and plans. This not only leads to a withdrawal of love units when the deception is discovered, it also makes marital conflicts impossible to resolve. As conflicts build, romantic love slips away.

You may agree with me that spouses should be honest with each other but you may wonder how far honesty should go. Before you give each other honesty as a Gift of Love, you should know precisely what should be included in your commitment. To help couples understand the extent of this gift, I have written a rule to guide them. It is the Rule of Honesty and it can be broken down into five parts:

1. *Emotional Honesty:* Reveal your emotional reactions—both positive and negative—to the events of your life, particularly to your spouse's behavior.
2. *Historical Honesty:* Reveal information about your personal history, particularly events that demonstrate personal weakness or failure.

3. *Current Honesty:* Reveal information about the events of your day. Provide your spouse with a calendar of your activities, with special emphasis on those that may affect your spouse.
4. *Future Honesty:* Reveal your thoughts and plans regarding future activities and objectives.
5. *Complete Honesty:* Do not leave your spouse with a false impression about your thoughts, feelings, habits, likes, dislikes, personal history, daily activities, or plans for the future. Do not deliberately keep personal information from your spouse.

The Rule of Honesty

Reveal to your spouse as much information about yourself as you know: your thoughts, feelings, habits, likes, dislikes, personal history, daily activities, and plans for the future.

To some extent this rule seems like motherhood and apple pie. Who would argue that it's *not* a good idea to be honest? But in my years of experience as a marriage counselor, I have found that many clients consider dishonesty a good idea under certain conditions.

To those who argue that dishonesty can be justified under certain circumstances, I must say that my Rule of Honesty leaves no room for exceptions. But because there are so many out there who *advocate* dishonesty in marriage, I need to build a case for my position. Let's take a careful look at each of the five parts of this rule, beginning with emotional honesty.

Emotional Honesty

Some people find it difficult to express their emotional reactions, particularly the negative ones. They may fear that others will judge them for their feelings or they may be judging themselves, telling themselves they should not feel the way they do. They may doubt their ability to express negative feelings without demands, judgments, or anger. Or, wanting unconditional acceptance from their spouse, they may think their negative reactions prove their own inability to be unconditionally accepting.

Emotional Honesty

Reveal your emotional reactions—both positive and negative—to the events of your life, particularly to your spouse's behavior.

But negative feelings serve a valuable purpose in a marriage. They are a signal that something is wrong. If you successfully steer clear of angry outbursts, disrespectful judgments, and selfish demands, your expression of negative feelings can alert both you and your partner to an adjustment that will make your marriage much more enjoyable.

Honesty enables a couple to make appropriate adjustments to each other. Adjustment is what a good marriage is all about. The circumstances that have led you into your blissful relationship will certainly change, and you will need to learn to adjust to them. Both of you are growing and changing with each new day and you must constantly adjust to each other's changes. But how can you know how to adjust if you're not receiving accurate information? That's flying blind, like a pilot whose instrument panel has shorted out.

You need a steady flow of accurate data from each other. Without this, unhappy situations can go on and on—like the flowers piling up in the allergic woman's home. But if you communicate your feelings to each other, you can correct what you're doing wrong before it becomes a habit.

The mere communication of feelings does not assure that all the necessary adjustments will be made. There is still work to do. But without that honest communication, failure is *guaranteed.*

Communication, of course, is a two-way street. Honest feelings need to be expressed and received. Complaints must be heard and honored. If you're getting the data, you must read it. But persistence is also important. Your commitment to honesty does not end when you have reported a feeling. You must continue to express feelings honestly to each other until the problem is resolved.

In other words, for honesty to take place in your relationship, you must allow each other to regularly express feelings, even if they have been expressed in the past. If you feel lonely frequently, express it frequently. Keep sending your message until you have found a solution to the problem. There is nothing wrong with expressing repeatedly your negative emotional reactions if the conflict that creates them has not been resolved.

But there is a difference between expressing your negative emotional reactions several times and nagging. The difference is Love Busters. Nagging adds your anger, disrespect, and demands to your honest expression. But when you express negative emotional reactions *without* Love Busters, you are fulfilling your commitment to honesty. Then you are simply telling your partner that a problem has not yet been resolved and the two of you need to keep thinking of solutions.

I've been discussing the difficulty and importance of expressing negative emotions, but I don't want to overlook the expression of positive feelings. While positive feelings are generally easier to communicate than negative ones, many couples have not learned to express these feelings either. Failing to do so, they miss an important opportunity to deposit love units. If you say clearly and enthusiastically that you like something your partner has done, you'll make your partner feel good, knowing that his or her care is appreciated.

Historical Honesty

Should your skeletons stay in the closet?

Some say yes: Lock the door, hide the key, leave well enough alone. Communicate your past misdeeds only on a need-to-know basis.

But I say your partner needs to know everything. Whatever embarrassing experiences or serious mistakes are in your past, you need to come clean with him or her.

Your personal history holds significant information about you, information about your strengths and weaknesses. For the one you are about to marry to make necessary adjustments to you, he or she needs to understand both your good and bad points. Where can you be relied on? Where do you need help?

For example, if a man has had problems controlling his temper in the past, it's likely he'll have the same struggle in the future. If a woman has been chemically dependent in the past, she'll be susceptible to drug or alcohol abuse in the future. If you talk openly about your past mistakes, your partner will understand your weaknesses, and together you can avoid situations that will tend to create problems for you in the future.

Historical Honesty

Reveal information about your personal history, particularly events that demonstrate personal weakness or failure.

No area of your life should be kept secret. All questions asked by your partner should be answered fully and completely. Periods of poor adjustment in your past should be given special attention. Be sure that both you and your partner understand what happened in those previous circumstances. That way you will be able to create a lifestyle together that does not tempt your weaknesses.

Not only should *you* explain your past to your partner, but you should encourage your partner to gather information from those who knew you before you met. I encourage couples who are considering marriage to talk with several significant people from each other's past. It's often quite an eye-opener.

The Rule of Historical Honesty demands that you disclose any of your past sexual relationships. You *must* confide in each other, regardless of the reaction, if you are to completely understand each other.

"But if I tell her about all the bad things I've done, she'll never trust me again."

"If he finds out about my past, he'll be crushed. It will ruin his whole image of me."

I have heard these protests from various clients, all ashamed of things they had done. Why dig it all up? Let old mistakes stay buried in ancient history! Why not just leave that little demon alone? I answer that it's not a "little demon," but an extremely important part of their personal story and it says something about their character.

Some believe that after marriage it's best not to reveal the sins of the past. Why put your spouse through the agony of a revelation that could ruin your relationship forever?

There are two answers to that question. The first answer is that your partner has a right to know the truth about you, regardless of how damaging it could be to your relationship. Truth is so important in marriage that it is worth risking marital failure.

But the second answer is that marriages are not ruined by honesty, they are ruined by dishonesty. It's far more likely that your partner will leave you after discovering that you've been dishonest about your past, than if you had been honest from the beginning. Furthermore, honesty will help prevent a repeat of past weaknesses, while dishonesty almost guarantees their intrusion into your marriage.

Maybe you don't really want to be known for who you are. That's the saddest position of all to be in. You'd rather keep your secret than experience one of life's greatest joys—to be loved and accepted in spite of known weaknesses.

You may be daunted by the idea of revealing your past, and that's understandable. But let me assure you that your relationship will be stronger for it. When you reveal the truth, there may be a negative reaction and some shaky times in your relationship, but if your relationship is a solid one, it will survive. If it doesn't, now is the time, before marriage, to discover that it's too weak to withstand difficulties. Dishonesty destroys intimacy, compatibility, and the feeling of love. Honesty promotes them. I've never seen a marriage destroyed by honesty.

Current Honesty

As an engaged couple, you are probably sharing your daily schedules with each other without giving it much thought. But after you are married, it will be easy to begin neglecting this important aspect of honesty.

Current Honesty

Reveal information about the events of your day. Provide your spouse with a calendar of your activities, with special emphasis on those that may affect your spouse.

In good marriages, couples become so interdependent that sharing a daily schedule is essential to their coordination of activities. In weak marriages, however, the partners are reluctant to reveal their schedules, because they often engage in activities that would offend each other. Assuming that their spouse would object to these activities, they hide the details of their day, telling themselves, *What he doesn't know won't hurt him* or *She's happier not knowing everything.*

Even when activities are innocent, it's extremely important for your partner to understand what you do with your time. Make sure you're easy to find in an emergency or when your partner just wants to say hello during the day. Give each other your daily schedule so you can communicate about how you spend your time. Almost everything you do will affect your partner, so it's important to explain what you do.

When the Policy of Joint Agreement and the Rule of Current Honesty are both followed, you will be able to create a life of marital compatibility. The two rules prevent the development of harmful habits and encourage a lifestyle that works well for both of you. The Policy of Joint Agreement helps you limit your habits and activities to those that are mutually enjoyable, and the Rule of Honesty prevents you from developing a secret second life where incompatible habits and activities are likely to flourish.

Future Honesty

After I've made such a big issue of revealing past indiscretions, you can imagine how I feel about revealing future plans that may get you into trouble. Future plans are much easier to discuss than past mistakes or failures, yet many couples keep their plans secret from each other. Why? Some people believe that communicating future plans just gives a spouse the opportunity to quash them. They have their sights set on a certain goal and they don't want anything to stand in their way.

When you fail to tell your partner about your plans, you're not being honest. You may be trying to avoid trouble in the present, but eventually the future will arrive, revealing your thoughtless plans. At that point your partner will be hurt that you didn't take his or her feelings into account when you were making those plans. And that will withdraw love units.

The Policy of Joint Agreement—*Never do anything without an enthusiastic agreement between you and your spouse*—is certainly relevant in discussions of your future plans.

Future Honesty

Reveal your thoughts and plans regarding future activities and objectives.

"If I wait for my wife to agree," a husband might say, "we'll never accomplish anything. She's so conservative; she never wants to take any risks, and so we miss every opportunity that comes along." But isn't that approach, in essence, a disrespectful judgment, forcing the husband's opinion on the wife? If he genuinely respects her, he will want her input on the decision—and more than mere input, her enthusiastic agreement!

"Oh, but the plans I make are best for both of us," a wife might say. "He may not understand my decision now but once he sees how things turn out, he'll thank me for going ahead with it." But to make plans independently and conceal them from your partner is still dishonest. Granted, you won't lose love units until later but you will lose them. Even if your plans work out, your spouse will still feel bad about not being included in the planning.

Complete Honesty

The time to practice being completely honest with each other is during the engagement period. If you get into the habit of hiding things now, that habit will continue after your marriage and endanger its vitality.

I ask probing questions during premarital counseling. And I probe most deeply in areas where people tend to leave false impressions. Since most marital problems originate with serious misconceptions, I do what I can to dig out these little weeds that eventually choke the plant.

It goes without saying that false impressions are just as deceitful as outright lies. The purpose of honesty is having the facts in front of you. Without them, you'll fail to solve the simplest marital problems. Lying to your spouse or giving false impressions will leave your spouse ignorant of the facts.

Complete Honesty

Do not leave your spouse with a false impression about your thoughts, feelings, habits, likes, dislikes, personal history, daily activities, or plans for the future. Do not deliberately keep personal information from your spouse.

In marriage one of the biggest false impressions may be that both spouses are doing an outstanding job meeting each other's needs. This form of deceit is often tempting early in marriage. There are some areas in which one or both of you are dissatisfied, but you don't want to appear unappreciative. You don't want to run the risk of withdrawing love units by expressing your dissatisfaction.

But as we saw earlier, you can minimize the loss of love units by expressing your concerns in nonthreatening, nonjudgmental ways. You can show appreciation for the effort made to meet your needs and then provide guidance to make that effort more effective.

Only the true expression of your feelings will help you find a solution to your problems. You cripple your spouse whenever you do not reveal the complete truth. You provide a map that leads to failure. Truth is the only map that leads to success.

Nine

UNDERSTANDING HONESTY

You have undoubtedly discussed the subject of honesty with each other and have probably agreed to be honest throughout your lives together. That's what most couples do. That's what my wife, Joyce, and I did when we were first married. In fact it was so important to us that we created a way to avoid any misunderstanding. If either of us asked the other a question "on your word," it meant no joking. The other person had to tell the truth. We still follow that approach today.

But as much as couples want an honest relationship, there are three important reasons that dishonesty sneaks into marriages: (1) protection, (2) avoiding trouble, and (3) compulsion. While the

excuses are very different for each type of dishonesty, the result is the same—the marriage suffers.

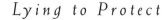

Lying to Protect

The most common type of dishonesty in marriage is motivated by protection. It hurts to be criticized, so spouses often avoid expressing their negative feelings toward each other, because they don't want to hurt each other. In other cases, people may protect their spouses from unpleasant information, perhaps a health scare or a financial setback.

I call these people "protector liars" and most of us fit this category, at least once in a while. Almost everybody can think of times when they have withheld their true feelings or the complete truth to avoid upsetting someone.

It seems quite innocent, doesn't it? Why upset your partner? Why ruin his or her good mood? But when you are being dishonest to protect your partner's feelings, it does far more than protect—it *denies* your partner crucial information. How would you feel if your bank stopped giving you monthly statements on your checking account, but continued to deduct fees without informing you? You'd be outraged. "When our customers run low in their accounts," the bank manager might say, "we try to protect them from that unpleasant information." It's crazy! That's exactly the time you *need* information, so you can make some deposits and avoid bouncing checks.

The same is true of you and your partner. You need to know when you are withdrawing love units, so you can make adjustments to prevent further loss. Without that information, you risk blindly drifting into Love Bank insolvency.

When you are experiencing negative feelings for your partner, you must let him or her know that withdrawals are taking place. That's the first step toward making the adjustments necessary to plug the leak in your Love Bank.

And when unpleasant financial or health information comes to your attention, why keep it from your partner? Do you have so little confidence in your partner that you don't believe he or she can handle it? That's not only disrespectful, but it prevents you from finding a solution to the crisis that meets with your partner's approval. It forces you to risk making a decision that you will later regret.

Lying to Avoid Trouble

Avoiding trouble is the second reason for dishonesty, arising from the fear of being caught doing something wrong. In marriage "avoiding-trouble liars" do things they know their spouse would not approve, so to avoid their spouse's judgment, they lie. Lies of this nature can be devastating to a marriage because they help one spouse create a secret second lifestyle that is totally incompatible with the feelings of the other spouse. Almost all of a marriage's most destructive habits grow in the hothouse of secret, carefully nurtured second lives.

Some people create this secret life, separate from the scrutiny of their spouse, because they are not willing to follow the Policy of Joint Agreement—they don't want to come to an enthusiastic agreement with their spouse before making a decision. Instead, they do what they please, knowing full well that their decision is not in their spouse's best interest. They don't lie because they're ashamed of their actions; they lie because it's a necessary part of keeping their secret lifestyle going. Since the spouse would not understand or accept the truth and would certainly cause a great deal of trouble if he or she discovered it, these liars simply avoid trouble by covering up their illicit deed. When the deed is discovered, the spouse is dealt a double blow—one is the lying spouse's failure to protect, and the other is his or her failure to be honest.

Born Liars

The third type of dishonesty is compulsion. Some people lie about anything and everything, whether they have a good reason or not. I call them "born liars." They don't seem to be able to control their lying, nor do they know why they do it. These people start lying from the time they can first talk. They often lie about personal experiences and accomplishments, and sometimes even convince themselves that the lies are true. Even evidence to the contrary does not always dissuade them.

Born liars almost always lead double lives. Occasionally you'll read a news story about some con artist who has finally been caught; usually people like this are born liars—passing themselves off as doctors or lawyers, or marrying two or more people at once. When caught in their crime, they sincerely deny any guilt and can even pass lie detector tests. Such liars are fascinating to psychologists like me but, for obvious reasons, are impossible as marriage partners. Since honesty is essential in marriage, and these individuals simply cannot tell the truth, their marriages are almost always very short-lived.

This third category, compulsion, is obviously the most severe form of dishonesty, and thankfully, very few of the spouses I counsel are born liars. If you and your partner ever face dishonesty in your marriage, it will probably be protective lying or avoiding-trouble lying. Fortunately these two patterns of lying can be overcome, but it is much more difficult for a compulsive liar to learn to be honest. In fact I have seen little improvement in a compulsive liar regardless of the type of therapy used.

Is Honesty a Love Buster?

Isn't honesty, in some cases, a Love Buster? Aren't there times when a couple can be *too* honest with each other, when it would be better to avoid conflict by keeping a spouse in the dark?

That's what many couples think. They assume their relationship would suffer harm if they expressed their true feelings. And, on the surface, this argument seems to make sense. Love Busters are those actions that make your spouse unhappy; so if your expression of honesty troubles your spouse, it's a Love Buster.

Not so fast. When you take a closer look, you find that the Love Buster isn't honesty itself, but the thing that honesty reveals. Confessing to an affair will certainly upset your spouse, but it isn't the confession that's upsetting, it's the affair!

In most cases, dishonesty merely postpones your spouse's discovery of the truth, and once it's revealed, the fact that you lied will do even more damage to your relationship. Then your spouse will be upset by the truth *and* your dishonesty. And of the two, your dishonesty will usually hurt your spouse more than whatever it was you were trying to conceal. Dishonesty in marriage, once discovered, causes incredible pain.

Don't Wrap Your Honesty in Love Busters

Can your expression of honesty actually be a Love Buster in disguise? What if you were to express your unhappiness by throwing a lamp and crying out, "You never have time for me anymore. I don't know why I ever married you, you selfish jerk"? You might get points for honesty but they'd all be lost because of your angry outburst. It does no good to express genuine feelings if your spouse is running for cover.

Instead of getting angry, you might say, "Your priorities are certainly screwed up. You seem to think that money is more important than I am. If you don't straighten out soon, you'll be sleeping with your money." That may be your honest opinion, but you are wrapping it in a disrespectful judgment. If your spouse is put on the defensive, he or she never really hears what you're saying. Whatever is gained by expressing your feelings is quickly lost in the Love Buster.

Some day you may have difficulty making a sexual adjustment. There's nothing wrong with an honest appeal for help, but if it turns out to be a demand, it's a Love Buster.

It's often not easy to express feelings while keeping angry outbursts, disrespectful judgments, or selfish demands in check. Anyone can learn to do it, though.

"I'm the least important person in your life. You'd rather be with anyone else but me" is a disrespectful judgment because you are telling your spouse how he or she feels. The truth is you don't know how your spouse feels, unless he or she tells you.

"I become upset when I'm left alone at night" is an honest statement of your feeling, because you are telling your spouse how *you* feel.

"If you don't start spending more time with me soon, I'll find someone else to spend time with" is a selfish demand.

"I'd like to spend more time with you" is an honest statement of feeling.

To be honest with your spouse, you must be willing to reveal your feelings, but you must reveal them in a way that helps your marriage and doesn't hurt it.

Encourage Each Other to Be Honest

You may say that you want honesty in your relationship, but in reality you may not encourage honesty all of the time. How do you answer the following questions?

1. If the truth would be terribly upsetting to you, do you want your partner to be honest with you only at times when you are emotionally prepared?
2. Do you keep some aspects of your life secret and do you encourage your partner to respect your privacy or boundaries in those areas?
3. Do you like to create a certain mystery between you and your partner?
4. Are there conditions under which you would not want honesty at all costs between you and your partner?

If you answer yes to any of these questions, you do not always value honesty. In certain situations, you feel your marriage is better off with dishonesty, or at least with something less than the truth. That little crack is all dishonesty needs to slip into your marriage and cause it to run amok. You see, there are always "reasons" to be dishonest. As soon as you allow one, they begin to blur into all the rest, and before you know it, you have a dishonest relationship.

You encourage honesty when you *value* honesty. If your own values do not consistently support honesty, you will be sending each other mixed messages that will undermine this third Gift of Love.

Having consistent values is one way to encourage honesty. But another important way to encourage it is in the way you react to honesty. Do your reactions convey an appreciation for the truth, even if it's painful? These questions will help you determine if you are actually discouraging honesty in the way you sometimes react to it.

1. Do you ever have angry outbursts when your partner is honest with you?
2. Do you ever make disrespectful judgments when your partner is honest with you?
3. Do you ever make selfish demands when your partner is honest with you?

If you answered yes to any of these questions, you are using Love Busters to punish honesty and are inadvertently encouraging dishonesty. The way to encourage each other to be truthful is to minimize the negative consequences of truthful revelations. Instead of trying to punish your partner when a shocking truth is revealed, try to reward your partner's honesty. Remember, honesty itself is never your enemy, it's a friend that brings light to a problem that often needs a creative solution. If honesty is followed by safe and pleasant negotiation, it becomes the necessary first step toward improvement in your compatibility and love for each other.

When you are on the receiving end of an honest disclosure, you come face to face with how difficult it is to reward honesty. When faced with the truth, some spouses react with rage. Some cry, some scream, some hit, some threaten—and all these things just convince their spouse to cover their crimes more carefully in the future. Don't make your partner miserable when he or she tells you the truth. That simply encourages dishonesty the next time. Instead, talk about how important honesty is to you and how you want to work together to achieve greater love and compatibility.

PART FOUR

The Gift of Time

I PROMISE TO TAKE TIME
TO GIVE YOU MY
UNDIVIDED ATTENTION

Ten

WHAT IS TIME?

The Gifts of Care, Protection, and Honesty are easily understood as being essential for marital health and happiness. They're not always given in marriage, but most of us know, deep down, that they *should* be given.

There is still one more gift that you and your partner should present to each other. This gift is not only more difficult to understand as being essential for your marital happiness, it is also more difficult to give than the other three. It is the Gift of Time.

As an engaged couple, you probably spend the majority of your leisure time together. And the time you spend together is the most enjoyable part of the day. Spending time alone with each other is your highest priority, and you may even cancel other plans when you have an opportunity to be together.

You probably try to talk to each other every day. If you can't physically be with each other, you talk on the telephone, sometimes for hours. And when you are together, you give each other your undivided attention.

If you are like most couples, you plan your time together. That way you can be together as much as possible. If you were together only when you both had nothing else to do, you probably wouldn't be together very often.

How much time do you usually spend with each other every week, physically or on the telephone? And during that time are you giving each other your undivided attention? If you are like most couples, your time together, either in person or by telephone, is about twenty-five hours a week and for at least fifteen of those hours you have each other's undivided attention.

I have done some investigating to discover common dating practices and I've been amazed at how much time is devoted to courtship, especially just prior to marriage. The results show that time spent together is directly proportional to whether or not a couple marries. The more time spent together, the more likely the marriage will take place. These results are not surprising since it takes quite a bit of time to deposit enough love units to trigger and sustain romantic love.

If you are like I was when I married my wife, Joyce, you want to be married so that you can spend even more time together. This scheduling business can be a real pain, and living together in marriage seems to be the perfect answer.

But unless you give each other the Gift of Time, you will find that after you are married, you will no longer give each other the undivided attention you gave before marriage. That's because most couples think that being together physically is the same as being together emotionally.

Before you marry, being together physically usually means you are also together emotionally. But after marriage, you will find that you can be in the same room together and yet ignore each other emotionally. What's even worse, you may find that you are not even in the same room together as much as you had expected to be, particularly after your children arrive.

One difficult aspect of marriage counseling is scheduling time for it. The counselor must often work evenings and weekends because most couples will not give up work for their appointments. Then the counselor must schedule around a host of evening and weekend activities that take the husband and wife in opposite directions.

Another difficult aspect of marriage counseling is arranging time for the couple to be together to carry out their first assignment. Many couples think that a counselor will solve their problems with a weekly conversation in his office. It doesn't occur to them that it's what they do after they leave the office that saves their marriage. To accomplish anything, they must schedule time to be together. This often turns out to be the most painful assignment—rearranging their schedule to include each other.

It's incredible how many couples have tried to talk me out of their spending more time together. They begin by trying to convince me that it's impossible. Then they go on to the argument that it's impractical. But in the end, they usually agree that without time they cannot possibly re-create the love they once had for each other.

To prevent you from making the common mistake of neglecting each other after marriage, I suggest that you follow the Rule of Time.

The Rule of Time has three important corollary rules having to do with privacy, objectives, and amount.

Corollary 1: Privacy. *The time you plan to be together should not include children, relatives, or friends. Establish privacy so that you are able to give each other your undivided attention.*

It's essential that you as a couple spend time alone. When you have time alone, you have a much greater opportunity to deposit love units into each other's Love Bank. With-

---

The Rule of Time

Give your spouse your undivided attention a minimum of fifteen hours each week, using the time to meet his or her most important emotional needs.

---

out privacy, undivided attention is almost impossible, and without undivided attention, you are not likely to meet some of each other's most important emotional needs.

First, I recommend that you learn to be together without your children. This is an easy assignment because you probably don't yet have children. But I'm amazed at how difficult an assignment this becomes after children arrive. Many couples don't think children interfere with their privacy. To them, an evening with their children *is* privacy. Of course, they know they can't make love with children around. But I believe that the presence of children prevents much more than lovemaking. When children are present, they interfere with affection and intimate conversation that are desperately needed in marriage.

Second, I recommend that friends and relatives not be present during your time together. This may mean that after everything has been scheduled, there's no time left over for friends and relatives. If that's the case, you're too busy, but at least you won't be sacrificing your love for each other.

Third, I recommend that you understand what giving undivided attention means. Remember, it's what you have done while dating. There's no way you would be planning to marry if you had ignored each other on dates. You look at each other when you are talking, you are interested in the conversation, and there is little to distract you. This is the undivided attention you must give each other as a married couple.

When you see a movie together, the time you're watching it doesn't count toward your time for undivided attention (unless you behave like the couple who sat in front of my wife and me last week!). It's the same with television or sporting events. You should engage in these recreational activities together, but the time I want you to commit yourselves to is very clearly defined—it's the time you pay close attention to each other.

Now that you're alone with each other, what should you do with this time? The second corollary of the Rule of Time deals with objectives.

Corollary 2: Objectives. *During the time you are together, create activities that will meet the emotional needs of affection, sexual fulfillment, conversation, and recreational companionship.*

Romance for most men is sex and recreation; for most women it's affection and conversation. When all four come together, men and women alike call it romance and they deposit the most love units possible. That makes these categories somewhat inseparable whenever you spend time together. My advice is to try to combine them all.

After marriage women often try to get their husband to meet their emotional needs for conversation and affection, without necessarily meeting their husband's needs for sex and recreational companionship. Men, on the other hand, want their wife to meet their needs for sexual fulfillment and recreational companionship, without meeting her needs for affection and conversation. Neither strategy works very well. Women often resent having sex without affection and conversation first, and men resent being attentive and affectionate with no hope for sex or recreation. By combining the needs into a single event, however, both spouses have their needs met, and enjoy the time together.

A man should never assume that just because he is in bed with his wife, sex is there for the taking. In many new marriages, that mistake is made and it creates resentment and confusion. Most men eventually learn that if they spend the evening giving their wife their undivided attention, with conversation and affection, sex becomes a very natural and mutually enjoyable way to end the evening.

But there are some women who don't see the connection either. They want their husband to give them the most attention when there is no possibility for sex. In fact knowing that affection and intimate conversation often lead a man to sex, they try hardest to be affectionate when they are out in a crowd. That tactic can lead to just as much resentment in a man as nightly sexual "ambushes" create in a woman. Take my word for it, the fulfillment of the four needs of affection, conversation, recreational companionship, and sexual fulfillment is best when they are met together.

Corollary 3: Amount. You will need to choose the number of hours to be together that reflects the quality of your marriage. If your marriage is satisfying to you and your spouse, plan to schedule fifteen hours each week for your undivided attention. But if you suffer marital dissatisfaction, plan more time, until marital satisfaction is achieved.

How much time do you need to sustain the feeling of romantic love? Believe it or not, there really is an answer to this question, and it depends on the health of a marriage. If a couple is deeply in love with each other and find that their marital needs are being met, I have found that about fifteen hours each week of undivided attention is usually enough to sustain romantic love. It is probably the least amount of time necessary. When a marriage is this healthy, either it's a new marriage or the couple has already been spending fifteen hours a week alone with each other throughout their marriage.

When I apply the fifteen-hour principle to marriages, I usually recommend that the time be evenly distributed through the week, two to three hours each day. When time must be bunched up—all hours on the weekend—good results are not as predictable. Spouses need to be emotionally reconnected almost on a daily basis to sustain their love for each other.

How can a workaholic businessman find time to have an affair? The man who couldn't be home for dinner because of his busy schedule is suddenly able to fit in mid-afternoon rendezvous three times a week. How does he get his work done? The answer, of course, is that he had the time all along. It's simply a matter of priorities. He could just as easily have taken the time with his wife. Then they would have been in love with each other. Instead, he's in love with someone else, all because of a shortsighted schedule.

The reasons I have so much difficulty getting couples to spend time alone together is that when I first see them for counseling, they're not in love. Their relationship doesn't do anything for them, and the time spent with each other seems like a total waste at first. But when they spend time together, they learn to re-create the romantic experiences that first nurtured their love relationship. Without that time, they have little hope of restoring the love they once had for each other. For them fifteen hours a week isn't enough. To jump-start the relationship, these marriages usually require twenty-five or thirty hours a week of undivided attention.

At this time you probably find it easy to schedule time to be with each other but as your responsibilities increase, especially after you have children, you will be tempted to make a great mistake. You will be tempted to stop giving each other your undivided attention and meeting each other's most important emotional needs. Don't do it. Your time together is too important to the security of your relationship. It's more important than time spent on anything else, including your children and your job. Remember that the time you should set aside is only equivalent to a part-time job. It isn't time you don't have; it's time you will use for something less important, if you don't use it for each other.

Eleven

SCHEDULING TIME
FOR UNDIVIDED ATTENTION

You're in love with each other because you have done such a good job meeting each other's emotional needs. You have been able to meet those needs because you give each other your undivided attention when you are together. Unless you continue to give each other that kind of attention throughout your marriage, you will not be able to meet each other's needs and you will lose your love for each other.

Picture a couple in a corner of a restaurant, having a romantic dinner together. Suddenly the husband's cell phone rings, and he talks on it for five minutes. After a while his wife begins to fume. This scene illustrates what's wrong with marriages these days. The husband thinks he should get credit for spending time with his wife, taking her out to dinner. What ruins it all is that he does not give her his undivided attention. The time they spend together does not meet her emotional needs; all it does is prove to her that she's not as important as the next call on the phone.

As soon as you are married, and especially after you have children, obstacles will appear that will prevent you from giving each other the undivided attention that you both need. You will find that as your life becomes more complex, you will try to accomplish several objectives at once, and when you spend time together, you will be thinking of other pressing problems that need to be solved.

The older you get, the more busy you will become. You will not be able to do everything you want. And if you are not careful, the things that are most important to you will get pushed aside by things that are less important but more urgent.

That's what makes a schedule so important. It helps you determine how you will spend your week before urgent demands start to pile up. Instead of mindlessly attending to every demand, you can decide in advance the worthiness of the effort and decline those that are less important.

Imagine having a lawn-mowing service that is so popular that people constantly call to have you care for their yards. But because so many people call, you never have a chance to get out of the house to mow any lawns. Regardless of the number of calls you get, you are unable to earn a living because you never leave the phone. It's always ringing, and you feel you must be there to answer it.

You can get just as sidetracked in your marriage. Just as a lawn-mowing business will go broke if you're too busy to mow any lawns, the love in your marriage will be lost if you don't have time to meet each other's important emotional needs. If you don't protect your time together, you will find that responsibilities of lesser value will fill it up.

Making a Schedule

Your love for each other cannot be created or sustained without time for undivided attention. And unless you schedule time to meet each other's emotional needs, it won't get done. As I mentioned earlier, setting aside time to give each other undivided attention is one of the most difficult assignments I can give you, not because you object to being with each other, but because the pressures of life usually crowd out the time it takes to sustain romantic love.

Schedule on your calendars at least fifteen hours a week during which you will give each other undivided attention. Decide what you will do during the time and write that in. Also set aside a time at the end of each week to evaluate how well you did.

Since we are creatures of habit, I recommend that the hours you spend alone together be at the same time each day, week after week. If you keep the same schedule every week, it will be easier to follow the Rule of Time.

The total amount of time you spend together doesn't necessarily affect the way you feel about each other in the week that the time is spent. It has more effect on the way you're *going to feel* about each other in future weeks. You're building Love Bank accounts when you spend enjoyable time together, and the account must build before you feel the effect.

From my perspective as a marriage counselor, the time you spend alone with each other is the most valuable of your week. It's the time when you are depositing the most love units and ensuring romantic love for your marriage. The goal each week is to guarantee each other enough time to meet each other's needs for affection, conversation, sexual fulfillment, and recreational companionship, needs that when met tend to deposit the most love units.

You won't have to write your schedule of time together in your calendars for the rest of your life, although it will probably be something you won't mind doing after you get into the habit. For the first few weeks of your marriage, however, write them in to help you get into some good habits. Then, once the habits are set and you are happy with the amount of time you spend with each other, you can forget about writing the dates in your calendars.

Make a bargain with each other that if either of you feels that your time together is deteriorating, you will get back to scheduling your dates on the calendar again. Spend time talking about how you're spending your time together. This will help you see what's gone wrong, discuss needed improvements in your behavior, and get into a new habit that solves a problem.

Recreational Companions

You must do more than just schedule time to be together and give each other undivided attention. As is now the case in your relationship, after marriage your time together should continue to be the most enjoyable time of the week for both of you. Until now it's been almost effortless to make your time together enjoyable. But after marriage, if you are not careful, it can become a burden. That's because you may not make good adjustments to each other's changing needs.

In every marriage, people change. What is enjoyable at twenty is often no longer fun at forty. So it's entirely possible that something both of you enjoy now will eventually become boring or even unpleasant to one of you. Couples often make the fatal mistake of going their separate ways when an activity becomes boring to one of them. After all, they reason, why make one spouse sacrifice an enjoyable activity just to accommodate the other? If one spouse has become skilled playing golf, for example, why give it up just because the other spouse has lost interest in the sport?

The answers to those questions depend on the importance of love in your marriage. If the love you have for each other is more important than your leisure activities, then you must spend your most enjoyable time with each other, and that time must be mutually enjoyable.

But if your leisure activities are more important than your love, then you should pursue your favorite activities independently of each other. If that's your choice, and if you don't spend your most enjoyable time together, you will lose your emotional bond and your love for each other. Those are strong words, but as someone who has spent his life trying to save marriages, I know what I'm talking about.

One of the easiest ways to deposit love units into each other's Love Bank is to enjoy leisure activities together. If you choose to spend your most enjoyable leisure time apart, however, you not only miss an opportunity to build mutual love, but someone else may deposit enough love units into your Love Bank to risk an affair.

Remember, your love for each other is more important than any leisure activity. That means that being with each other recreationally is more important than the particular activity you choose to do together. Why? It's because the purpose of the activity is to help build your relationship. It's not the other way around. The purpose of your being together is not to improve your skill in a particular recreational activity. You are not marrying each other because you enjoy playing tennis together. You play tennis together because it's a way of building your love for each other.

If your spouse decides he or she doesn't enjoy tennis anymore, don't risk damaging your relationship by going off and playing tennis by yourself. Find an alternative to tennis that will be just as enjoyable for both of you.

It's extremely important to be each other's best friend throughout life. You do that by making each other a part of every enjoyable activity you have. If it's fun to do, your spouse should do it with you. If your spouse doesn't enjoy doing it, give it up. Whatever activity you choose—jogging, bicycling, playing softball, golfing—be sure your spouse wants to do it too. Don't develop skills in an activity that your spouse does not enjoy.

The saying, "If you're not with the one you love, love the one you're with," did not come from nowhere. It's the rule thousands use to meet their emotional needs. If you have a job that takes you away from your spouse, you will both be vulnerable to an affair. At one time I just about completely supported myself and my family counseling airline pilots, because pilots and their wives tend to have affairs when they are not with each other. Those in the military also keep marriage counselors busy for the same reason.

But jobs that separate spouses for weeks, or even days at a time, are not the only cause of affairs. Recreational activities that separate spouses can also encourage affairs. You may be together every day of the week but if you choose to become recreationally separated, you sacrifice what probably convinced you to marry—the good times you had together and your friendship.

Spend as much of your leisure time together as possible. It is not only one of the best ways to build your relationship, but it will also help you experience the most interesting and enjoyable parts of your life together. One of the quickest ways to become bored with each other is to have more interesting things to do when you are apart. Eliminate that destructive possibility by deliberately spending your most enjoyable moments with each other.

Twelve

FOR THE LOVE OF YOUR LIFE

When you exchange rings at your wedding, you now know what promises they will symbolize. As you put the rings on each other's finger, you will be giving each other the four gifts of love.

The Gift of Care

I promise to meet your most important emotional needs.

When a couple marry, they promise to care for each other. But few ever understand what that means. What have they actually promised to do?

You have a great advantage over most couples preparing for marriage—you now understand what care requires. Care is meeting each other's most important emotional needs.

It's likely that you and your partner do not prioritize your needs in the same order of importance. A highly important need for you may not be as important to your partner. So to fulfill your Gift of Care, you must learn to become an expert in meeting needs whether or not they seem important to you. Your partner will depend on you to meet those needs.

The Gift of Protection

I promise to avoid being the cause of your unhappiness.

After you are married and you become experts at meeting each other's important emotional needs, you will be the cause of each other's greatest happiness. But unless you do something to prevent it, you can also become the cause of each other's greatest unhappiness. That's why the Gift of Protection is so important.

You and your spouse were both born to be angry, disrespectful, demanding, annoying, and dishonest. These are normal human traits that I call Love Busters because they destroy the feeling of love couples have for each other. But if you promise to avoid being the cause of your partner's unhappiness, you will do whatever it takes to overcome these destructive tendencies for your partner's protection. By eliminating Love Busters, you will not only be protecting your partner, you will also be preserving your partner's love for you.

Almost everything you do will affect each other. So it's very important to know what that effect will be. The Policy of Joint Agreement will help you remember how much your decisions affect each other and how you must consult with each other to be sure you avoid being the cause of each other's unhappiness. By making mutually acceptable choices, you will create a lifestyle that both of you will enjoy.

The Gift of Honesty

I promise to be honest with you.

Your promise to be honest requires you to be honest about your feelings, your personal history, your current activities and experiences, and your future plans. It is *complete* honesty.

It won't be easy for you to keep your promise to be honest. Honesty is an unpopular value these days, and most couples have not made this commitment to each other.

Most marriage counselors and many clergymen argue that honesty is not always the best policy. They believe that it's cruel to disclose past indiscretions and it's selfish to make such disclosures. While it makes you feel better to get a mistake off your chest, it causes your partner to suffer. So, they argue, the truly caring thing is to lie about your mistakes or at least keep them tucked away.

And if it's compassionate to lie about the sins of the past, why isn't it also compassionate to lie about sins of the present—or future? To my way of thinking, it's like letting the proverbial camel's nose into the tent. Eventually you will be dining with the camel. Either honesty is always right, or you'll always have an excuse for being dishonest.

Self-imposed honesty with your partner is essential to your marriage's safety and success. Honesty will not only bring you closer to each other emotionally, it will also prevent the creation of destructive habits that are kept secret from your partner. The Rule of Honesty combined with the Policy of Joint Agreement are two guidelines that will help you create an open and integrated lifestyle, one that will guarantee your love for each other.

The Gift of Time

I promise to take time to give you my undivided attention.

The Gift of Time unlocks the door to the other three gifts. Without it, you will not be able to meet each other's emotional needs nor will you be able to avoid being the cause of each other's unhappiness. Time is also a basic requirement for honesty. Time for undivided attention is the necessary ingredient for everything that's important in your marriage.

And yet, as soon as you are married and especially when children arrive, you will find yourselves tempted to replace your time togther with activities of lesser importance. You will try to meet each other's needs with time "left over," but sadly, there won't be any time left over. Your lack of private time together will become a great cause of unhappiness, and yet you will feel that you are incapable of preventing it. You will also find yourselves bottling up your honest expression of feelings because there is just no appropriate time to talk.

Schedule your time to be alone with each other as your highest priority—that way it will never be replaced by activites of lesser value. Your career, time with your children, maintenance of your home, and a host of other demands will all compete for your time together. But if you promise each other the Gift of Time, you will not let anything steal from you those precious hours together.

Agreement to Meet the Most Important Emotional Needs

This Agreement is made this _____ day of _____ , _____ ,

between _____ and _____ ,

whereby it is mutually agreed:

_____ will learn to meet the following emotional
(Husband's name)

   needs of _____ :
(Wife's name)

1. _____

2. _____

3. _____

4. _____

5. _____

_____ will learn to meet the following emotional
(Wife's name)

   needs of _____ :
(Husband's name)

1. _____

2. _____

3. _____

4. _____

5. _____

   In Witness Whereof, the parties hereto have signed this agreement on the day and year first

above written:

_____   _____
His signature   Her signature

Agreement to Overcome Love Busters

This Agreement is made this _____ day of _____ , _____ ,

between _____ and _____ ,

whereby it is mutually agreed:

_____ will learn to avoid the following Love Busters:
               (Husband's name)

     1. _____

     2. _____

     3. _____

     4. _____

     5. _____

_____ will learn to avoid the following Love Busters:
               (Wife's name)

     1. _____

     2. _____

     3. _____

     4. _____

     5. _____

     In Witness Whereof, the parties hereto have signed this agreement on the day and year first above written:

_____   _____

His signature   Her signature

About the Author

Willard F. Harley, Jr., Ph.D., is a clinical psychologist and marriage counselor. Over the past twenty-five years he has helped thousands of couples overcome marital conflict and restore their love for each other. His innovative counseling methods are described in the books and articles he writes. He also leads training workshops for couples and appears regularly on radio and television.

Dr. Harley and Joyce, his wife of thirty-five years, live in White Bear Lake, Minnesota. They are parents of two married children who are also marriage counselors.

Be sure to visit Dr. Harley's web site at http://www.marriagebuilders.com.